CONTENTS

ACKNOWLEDGEMENTS

The authors and publishers are grateful to the following for permission to reproduce previously published and copyright material:

- The Open University Press for the diagram of the play spiral (p. 36), reproduced from Moyles, J., *Just Playing? The role and status of play in early childhood education*, Open University Press, 1989.
- Nottinghamshire Local Education Authority for the Entry and Baseline Assessment form (pp. 76–7).
- Weinberger, J., Hannon, P. and Nutbrown, C., for permission to reproduce the Reading Skills jigsaw (p. 78) from 'Ways of Working with Parents to Promote Early Literacy Development', USDE Papers in Education No. 14, University of Sheffield.
- Ron Adams for the photographs on pp. 121, 152 and 159.

Every attempt has been made to contact copyright holders, and we apologise if any have been overlooked.

GOOD PRACTICE IN IMPLEMENTING THE PRE-SCHOOL CURRICULUM

Sally Neaum ● **Jill Tallack**

Stanley Thornes (Publishers) Ltd

First published in 1997 by:
Stanley Thornes (Publishers) Ltd
Ellenborough House
Wellington Street
CHELTENHAM GL50 1YW
England

97 98 99 00 / 10 9 8 7 6 5 4 3 2

A catalogue record for this book
is available from the British Library.

ISBN 0-7487-2882-1

Typeset by Columns Design Ltd, Reading
Printed and bound in Great Britain by Redwood Books, Trowbridge, Wiltshire

INTRODUCTION

Good Practice in Implementing the Pre-school Curriculum examines issues around the development of a pre-school curriculum for three- to five-year-olds, particularly in the light of recent initiatives. It has been written with the needs of practitioners from a wide variety of pre-school settings in mind and aims to support the development of the curriculum into practice. The contents of this book also relate to the curriculum modules of the CACHE Diploma in Nursery Nursing and the Advanced Diploma in Childcare and Education, as well as to elements of the BTEC Nursery Nursing and HNC in Early Childhood Studies programmes. The book provides underpinning knowledge for some units of the NVQ awards in Childcare and Education and students on other courses that have a component on the pre-school curriculum may also find the book useful.

The authors recognise that there is controversy over the setting down of curriculum objectives for pre-school-aged children. However their intention is to match these initiatives against the wealth of existing good practice in this field.

This book provides practical examples, illustrated by case studies, of how establishments can develop a framework for the curriculum (guidance on which was issued by the Department for Education and Employment in 1996) within which the desirable outcomes of the guide can be achieved. It acknowledges that the desirable outcomes are part only of a much broader set of objectives for the pre-school curriculum.

For ease of explanation, this book looks at each of the areas of the Desirable Outcomes curriculum separately. However, it should be emphasised that young children learn most effectively from an integrated approach that takes into account the child's whole range of needs. Therefore, the book's starting point is that all children are individuals and that any establishment will seek to cater for the full range of needs.

Using the book

This book is presented in two parts. Part one gives a historical overview of the pre-school curriculum which puts recent initiatives into their context and also addresses, in some detail, aspects of good, professional practice. In part two, each chapter deals with a curriculum area as described in the Desirable Outcomes document and looks at providing for each aspect of the requirements.

There are features that are used throughout the book. Each chapter begins with a list of the main areas that are covered. Case studies are used to illustrate many aspects of the material discussed and questions are posed at the end of each case study which ask you to think about what you have read and perhaps apply it to other situations.

Throughout the chapters, pointers to good practice are identified and emphasised. At the end of each section there are questions, which check your progress, asking you to recap on what you have just read. Each chapter has a list of key terms at the end and some have further reading that is specific to the content of the chapter. The glossary at the end of the book provides a brief explanation of many of the key terms. A more extensive further reading list and a list of useful addresses are provided at the back of the book.

PART ONE
The Learning Framework

CURRICULUM PERSPECTIVES

Development of the pre-school curriculum

Provision for the education of pre-school children has developed and changed with the increasing understanding of children's behaviour and how they learn. Particularly influential in developing the views we have of children, their learning and the early education process, that are currently reflected in pre-school provision, were Friedrich Froebel (1782–1852), Maria Montessori (1869–1952), Margaret Macmillan (1860–1931) and Susan Isaacs (1885–1948). The psychologist Jean Piaget (1896–1980) has also had a profound impact upon our understanding of how children learn (see chapter two, 'The learning process').

From these early influences we have developed an understanding of childhood as a stage in itself rather than as incomplete adulthood. It is now widely recognised, based in part upon the work of these influential educationalists, that children's thoughts, feelings and learning patterns are qualitatively different to adults'. Children's intrinsic motivation to learn and the necessity for active involvement with their learning environment are fundamental concepts in our understanding of early learning. It is on these concepts that we base and form the learning framework for pre-school-aged children. The particular influence of each of these educationalists is outlined below.

The Rumbold Committee's findings reflect the early-years tradition of a developmentally appropriate learning framework. Further links with the Desirable Outcomes guidance can be seen in their conclusions on appropriate curriculum content for the under-fives. They recognised that the process of education – how children learn – is inseparable from the content of education – what children learn. Within this context they produced guidelines for developing the curriculum content for under-fives. It is important to be aware that some early-years educators believe that curriculum content for pre-school-aged children should be wholly child-centred. In this definition of curriculum content a rich, stimulating environment is provided and children are allowed to follow their own interests, free from adult direction. The content of the curriculum thus arises out of the child's interests and abilities. The idea of pre-defining curriculum content, in terms of knowledge and skills to be acquired, is difficult to reconcile with this stance.

The Rumbold Report outlines eight areas of learning, appropriate for pre-school-aged children, that have informed the development of the areas of learning for the Desirable Outcomes.

- Aesthetic and creative – includes art, craft, design, music, dance and drama.
- Human and social – concerned with people, both now and in the past, and how they live(d).
- Language and literacy – includes speaking, listening, reading and writing.
- Mathematics – includes learning about shape, space and position, patterns and relationships, and comparison (measures and numerical).
- Physical – includes the development of manipulative and motor skills, physical control, coordination and mobility. It involves knowledge of how the body works and establishes positive attitudes towards a healthy and active way of life.
- Science – includes enabling children to use all their senses to observe carefully, notice patterns, predict outcomes and test their ideas. Throughout these activities opportunities for discussion, questioning and recording by drawing, painting and modelling are crucially important.
- Spiritual and moral – concerned with developing an understanding about the significance and quality of human life, the development of self-confidence and a sense of right and wrong.
- Technology – includes designing and making activities and the use of electronic equipment such as calculators, computers, programmable toys and keyboards.

It can, therefore, be seen that contemporary early childhood education is underpinned by a range of guiding principles about the characteristics of young children and the ways in which they think and learn. From this has emerged some agreement about appropriate curriculum content. The Early Years Curriculum Group (1995) summarise the guiding principles as follows.

- Early childhood is valid in itself, and is part of life, not simply a preparation for work, or for the next stage of education.
- The whole child is considered to be important – social, emotional, physical, intellectual and moral development are interrelated.
- Learning is holistic and for the young child it is not compartmentalised under subject headings.
- Intrinsic motivation is valuable because it results in child-initiated activity.

- Autonomy and self-discipline are emphasised.
- In the early years children learn best though firsthand experiences.
- What children *can* do, not what they cannot do, is the starting point in their education.
- There is potential in all children which emerges powerfully under favourable conditions.
- The adults and children to whom the child relates are of central importance.
- The child's education is seen as an interaction between the child and the environment, which includes people as well as materials and knowledge.

PROGRESS CHECK

1 What has influenced development and change in the pre-school curriculum?

2 Outline the concepts on which we base and form the learning framework for pre-school-aged children.

3 Outline the beliefs and contributions to the understanding of young children's learning of Froebel, Montessori, Macmillan and Isaacs.

4 How are these beliefs and contributions reflected in current provision?

5 Read through the principles that underpin current mainstream provision. Identify where and how these principles are reflected in your practice.

The diversity of mainstream pre-school provision

There is, at present, no national structure for the care and education of pre-school-aged children. The aim of the Desirable Outcomes is to standardise provision within establishments. Where and by whom the curriculum is delivered depends entirely upon local provision. Some early-years settings are primarily care establishments and others are primarily educational establishments. These are not, however, mutually exclusive and all early-years settings will have much in common. Listed below are the main types of early-years settings available to parents/carers. It is important to note that these outlines are general and local practice will vary.

LEA funded nursery

These are nursery classes, units and schools funded by the local education authority that are free to parents in the same way as is compulsory schooling. They are primarily providers of pre-school education and are staffed by qualified teachers and trained nursery nurses. Their hours are based on a school day and the duration of sessions are defined by the establishment.

LEA funded places in school

Some schools and/or local authorities have admission policies that mean that four-year-old children are in a school reception class. This is discretionary as children are not legally required to be in school until the term after their fifth birthday. As with all schooling this provision is primarily educational. Classes are staffed by qualified teachers sometimes with a trained nursery nurse. Children attend for the normal school day.

Private schools

Some parents/carers choose to send their children to schools outside the system provided by the state. These private nursery schools are registered with the DfEE (Department for Education and Employment) and are, therefore, primarily providers of education. Parents have to pay the full cost of sending their children to these schools. Staffing is a matter for each school to decide individually.

Social services funded nursery

These are nurseries funded by the local authority through the social services. They are free to parents who are offered a place. They are staffed by qualified nursery nurses. Many places are allocated to children in need and, therefore, they combine care and education. Many of these establishments also work with parents to develop their parenting skills. As with LEA funded nurseries the duration of the sessions and the day are defined by the establishment.

Private day nursery

These are nurseries owned by an individual or company. They are registered with the local social services to ensure that they comply with the law in terms of their provision. They are primarily care establishments in that they provide care for children usually while parents/carers are at work. They also, of course, provide play opportunities for children. Staffing will vary from establishment to establishment but there must, by law, be some qualified nursery nurses among the staff. The length of the day is usually defined by the establishment and parents/carers choose the length of the session(s) to suit their needs. Parents have to meet the full cost of their child's attendance at these nurseries.

Workplace nursery

These are nurseries provided by employers as a benefit for their staff. They are registered and inspected by social services agencies. Staffing will have to meet legal requirements which means that there will be some qualified nursery nurses among the staff. These are primarily care establishments although play activities will be provided. The length of day, sessions and access to the setting will be defined by each workplace and will vary from setting to setting.

Playgroups

Playgroups are provided by local people often in local halls and community centres. They often do not have a designated building and all the equipment is stored and set out at each session. They are registered with social services to ensure that their provision meets minimum requirements. The playgroup leader often has a PLA (Pre-school Learning Alliance) qualification and the other staff are volunteers. They provide play opportunities for children in a group setting. Playgroup sessions are usually half a day and children attend as they choose and/or as places allow. Parents/carers pay for the sessions, although this is usually a nominal amount.

Current developments in the pre-school curriculum

There has been a marked increase in the numbers of children attending some form of pre-school establishment. There are two main reasons for this:
- an increased awareness of the benefits of pre-school education
- the economic and social changes that have resulted in more parents working full-time and needing childcare facilities.

Providing pre-school care and education is expensive and because of these heavy financial demands, for both local education authorities and for parents/carers, it has become a political issue. There is, therefore, a move towards putting more public money into pre-school education. To ensure that what is provided is appropriate to pre-school-aged children a curriculum has been developed, in consultation with early childhood professionals, that must be provided in all establishments wishing to get government funding. This curriculum is the Desirable Outcomes.

It is important to note that for inspection purposes, linked to the funding, no distinction is made between providers. So a private nursery will be assessed by the same criteria as a nursery school and a playgroup. All will be expected to provide the full curriculum.

THE DESIRABLE OUTCOMES CURRICULUM

The pre-school curriculum is based upon a series of desirable outcomes that embody current mainstream good practice. The expectation is that the education programme provided within an establishment will enable children to reach the outcomes by their compulsory school age at five. The learning programme within

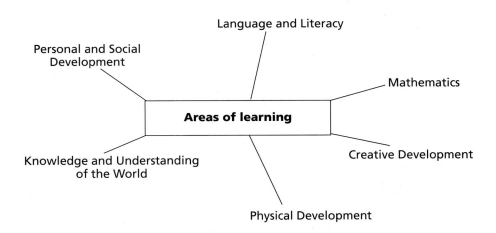

The Desirable Outcomes curriculum areas of learning

an establishment should be planned to enable children to develop their skills and concepts.

The outcomes are divided into six separate areas that correspond to the nine areas of learning adopted by the Rumbold Committee (1990): Personal and Social Development; Language and Literacy; Mathematics; Knowledge and Understanding of the World; Physical Development; Creative Development.

Each area has a statement of the skills and concepts that young children need to develop. For example:

> *Physical Development. Children move confidently and imaginatively with increasing control and co-ordination and an awareness of space and others. They use a range of large and small equipment and balancing and climbing apparatus, with increasing skill. They handle appropriate tools, objects, construction and malleable materials safely and with increasing control.*
> (Desirable Outcomes for Children's Learning, *DfEE with SCAA, 1996*)

Establishments must be able to demonstrate that their provision should enable children to achieve these outcomes by the time they reach compulsory school age. There is no formal assessment of the children required in the Desirable Outcomes curriculum. However it is expected that establishment-based assessment of individual children will be an important part of the provision. This should be evidenced by planning that is related to the Desirable Outcomes and informed by these evaluations of individual children. Practice should be clearly linked to planning. These aspects of provision are assessed during inspection.

MOVING ON TO THE NATIONAL CURRICULUM

One of the aims of the Desirable Outcomes is to lay the foundations for later learning. For most children their later schooling will be based on the National Curriculum. Some knowledge of the National Curriculum, therefore, provides a perspective on children's continuing education.

All state schools (funded by the government) are obliged by law to provide the National Curriculum. Private (fee paying) schools are not obliged by law to provide it but most do. The National Curriculum has a number of distinguishing features, some of which are significantly different to the Desirable Outcomes. It is a prescriptive curriculum, issued centrally, that covers the whole curriculum and each child must follow the curriculum.

The National Curriculum is divided into attainment targets that are statements of the outcomes to be achieved at specific stages in a child's schooling. These stages are referred to as Key Stages and are numbered 1 to 4. Key Stage 1 is for 5–7 year-olds, KS2 for 8–11 year-olds, KS3 for 12–14 year-olds and KS4 for 15–16 year-olds and GCSE level.

At each Key Stage, children must do a series of Standard Assessment Tasks (SATs). Individual children achieve a level of attainment according to the result of their standard assessment tasks (SATS) and, at Key Stage 1, teacher assessment. The levels of attainment achieved by an individual child are designed to indicate the child's individual progress through the curriculum.

PROGRESS CHECK

1 Why has there been an increase in the number of children attending pre-school establishments?

2 How do the authorities intend to ensure that provision is appropriate to pre-school children?

3 What are the differences between the Desirable Outcomes and the National Curriculum?

Inspection linked to the Desirable Outcomes

To become validated to accept government funding, establishments need to prove that they are providing the Desirable Outcomes curriculum. This is done through inspection. Every setting that wishes to accept government funding will have to be inspected. The aim of the inspection is to assess whether the education programme provided is likely to promote the desirable outcomes in each of the six areas of learning. This is important. Assessment will be based upon the planning, content, delivery and assessment of the educational programme and not upon individual children.

For inspection purposes no distinction is made between different types of establishment. All are assessed by the same criteria in all areas. Inspection, within the establishment will usually last for one day. In addition to this inspectors will spend some time preparing for the inspection and writing up the inspection report.

THE INSPECTION PROCESS

Before the inspection, the inspector will contact the establishment to set up an inspection date and outline the information and documentation that is required to prepare for the inspection. The information that is to be provided before the inspection is as follows:

- *a completed form giving details about the establishment*
- *a completed copy of the self-appraisal schedule*
- *the information that the establishment publishes for parents*
- *the policy and arrangements for children who have special educational needs*
- *any other policy documents that are available*
- *where applicable, the last inspection report*
- *a programme or timetable of the work that the establishment will be doing during the week of the inspection and, in particular, during the time of each inspection visit*
- *any other information that the establishment wishes to be considered*

(Guide for Inspectors, *OFSTED, 1996*)

Once this information has been read and understood by the inspector further discussions will take place to clarify how the inspectors will spend their time during the inspection visit and to outline the inspection process.

Other pre-school curriculum models

It is important to be aware that within the education system there is a range of curricula used within different establishments. The Desirable Outcomes is one of a number of pre-school curricula within the system. As it is to be implemented in many establishments linked with government funding, the majority of children will be involved in that curriculum.

Many of the curricula have much in common. All are based on the notion that children learn through active involvement with their environment and that this is best achieved through play. All acknowledge that childhood is a sensitive learning time and that children are highly receptive to all experiences. Where they differ is in their emphasis on particular aspects of pre-school experiences. For example the Steiner education curriculum is based upon a strong belief in the importance of the child's inner world of fantasy and creativity, therefore, the curriculum provided within Steiner schools reflects this.

An understanding of these curricula gives childcare workers a broader perspective of their own practice. In this context a number of other curricula are outlined here. The outline given is based upon the original philosophies and theories and provides an overview of the fundamental aspects of a curriculum and classroom experiences within that curriculum. As with all curricula there is an evolutionary process where ideas grow and change with experience so there will be some differences in implementation of these ideas within different establishments.

STEINER EDUCATION – THE WALDORF SCHOOLS

Steiner education is based on the educational philosophy of Rudolph Steiner. He believed in an education that allowed the individual child's impulses and talents to unfold; that education should, therefore, be free from the demands of the state and economic life; and that the fundamental goal of education is to awaken and cultivate the social capabilities of liberty, equality and fraternity. His view runs contrary to the mainstream understanding of education of developing skills that are required by society for its social, political and economic growth. Steiner believed that through education towards freedom for the individual, new forces could be brought to bear upon the existing social order. The social order would then be alive rather than reduced to conformity passed from one generation to another. Central to his system of education is the question, 'What gifts does an individual possess and how can they be developed?' rather than the more mainstream question, 'What does this person need to know to be able to fit into the existing social order?' (Carlgren, 1972).

The pre-school child, he believed, is a sense organ, reacting to his or her surroundings. Therefore, children learn through what happens all around them and not through didactic teaching. The physical environment in which children grow up is, therefore, of vital importance, but of equal importance are the child's experiences and interactions with other people.

Steiner strongly believed in the importance of a child's inner world, the ability to use fantasy and creativity and in the importance of the integration of mind and body in the learning process.

The pre-school child

Up to seven years is the age of imitation. At this age words are of little importance compared to the events and experiences in a child's life. Children are alert to all that goes on around them and the information is assimilated through vibrant sensual experience. Steiner wrote 'all that you do reverberates in a child' (Carlgren, 1972).

The pre-school years form the pattern for the child's growth and development. Therefore, they are vital years in a child's life. If what Steiner termed 'true forms' are developed in this first life period then true forms will grow. Conversely, if misshapen forms are developed, misshapen forms will grow. He believed that we can never repair what has been neglected during these initial years (Carlgren, 1972).

The kindergarten years – little material, much fantasy

Creative fantasy is a very important aspect of the kindergarten years. Through fantasy each child can discover and express their inner self, so the Steiner method encourages the development of powers of self-expression through a range of activities such as drawing, dancing, movement and music.

Toys that are provided should also allow fantasy as much rein as possible. Children should be able to develop their own play themes and ideas rather than the toys dictating their play through being designed to do only one thing. Play with junk items, boxes, planks, covers and cloths, twigs, stones, paper and containers should thus be encouraged.

As children sense and imitate what goes on in their environment it must be carefully considered. This includes the physical environment and the type and nature of the things that the child is coming into contact with:

- conditions of light and colour should be considered
- the room should be pleasing to a child, with beautiful furniture
- there should be as few finished products as possible to allow the child freedom to pretend
- items should be made from natural materials where possible
- plenty of paper, pens and modelling clay should be provided
- natural playthings such as twigs, stones, shells, cloth, wool, yarn, paper and wood should be provided, again to allow children the scope for imaginative play
- large boxes, wood, carpets and cloth provide for role play without being didactic
- children should come into contact with the natural world through a garden where they are involved in tending the plants and harvesting and using the natural products.

'Eurythmy', or eurhythmics – whole body rhythmical movement – forms part of children's experiences throughout kindergarten and beyond. At kindergarten level it is usually linked to stories, songs, poems and music. Children are encouraged to express their creative fantasy through their body movements.

To allow children freedom to express their own creative fantasy the adult's role is one of provider and guide. The adult does not initiate the play but becomes involved where appropriate. Strict and enforced discipline is absolutely minimal in the kindergarten years, as Steiner believed that children learn through imitation and interaction. Therefore, adults' good behaviour towards one another and towards the children is vital as children pick up on all that is going on within their environment. These experiences are perceived by the child and understood as acceptable behaviour.

MONTESSORI

Montessori education is named after its founder Maria Montessori who formed her ideas through her work as a doctor and psychiatrist and implemented these ideas initially with children living in difficult social conditions. Through working with the children and observing them carefully she developed a particular view of the best way for children to learn which she incorporated into her method.

The child is central in the Montessori method. Montessori concluded that childhood could be a frightening place where adults seem strong and powerful and children weak and powerless. This powerlessness was apparent in adults' always directing children's actions and responses. This, she believed, led to later difficulties and, therefore, children needed the opportunity to be able to decide for themselves and follow their own choices. She believed that children learned through their own spontaneous activity. Her ideas were built upon her observations that children have a natural inquisitiveness and eagerness to learn and she argued that children reached a sensitive learning time where certain skills and concepts are learned more readily. The opportunity to develop these concepts, therefore, should not be missed and a planned environment was necessary, she believed, to achieve this. Play, she argued, is a child's work.

Montessori, like Steiner, believed that the environment in which a child grows and develops is of great importance. Children's houses should be houses with different rooms and a garden. They should have child-sized furniture, be bright and light and appealing with rugs, pictures and flowers.

The Montessori classroom

The classroom is on a child's scale: small tables and chairs, a long low cupboard so that children can select their chosen activity, blackboards low enough for the children to write on them and rugs so that the children can sit on the floor. The classroom is bright and light with pictures on the walls and flowers around the room.

At its outset, learning within a Montessori classroom was controlled by the didactic materials that were central to this method of education. The didactic materials and activities were designed around the blocks, beads, cylinders and rods provided for the children to play with. Experimentation with these materials allowed the child to discover how and why things worked. There was no time limit to this exploration, children continued until satisfied. In order to achieve this the materials were:

- simple – though not easy – so that the child could understand them and the teacher could observe when to become involved
- inherently interesting
- self checking – so that the child knew whether he/she had succeeded or not without adult intervention.

These didactic materials still form part of the Montessori curriculum but many of today's Montessori schools have a curriculum that incorporates a broader range of experiences.

The adult's role in the curriculum, one of director, is to indirectly keep the children's interest through guiding, withdrawing and observing. The child will, therefore, see the adult as a friend, guide and helper who allows the child to do things for him/herself. In this way a child will develop a strong sense of independence and self confidence. The director observes the children and notes each child's stages of development. This will determine which are suitable activities. The child will then be guided by the director as to the most developmentally appropriate way of using the materials.

Discipline, in a traditional sense of strong adult and weak child, is limited to a few ground rules. Montessori believed that children would find their own level and, therefore, intervention by a director occurs when children's behaviour interferes with others.

High Scope

The High Scope curriculum was designed as a pre-school interventionist programme aiming to alleviate the perceived needs of children who were predicted as likely to fail within the education system. It is one of many such programmes developed in the USA. In the British education system implementation of the High Scope curriculum has not been according to the initial criteria but many establishments have implemented the curriculum as a system that embodies good pre-school practice.

The High Scope curriculum has a particular pattern of expectations, roles, structures and systems. Within this structure many of the familiar features of pre-school curriculum are evident – sand, water, painting, role play, construction and outdoor play.

The curriculum is based upon a range of psychological, educational and sociological theories. The underpinning psychological theory owes much to Piaget: that children learn best from active involvement with their environment. This is interpreted within an educational context in a learning-through-play approach which ensures that the curriculum is developmentally appropriate (see chapter two).

The sociological basis of the High Scope curriculum is the now generally accepted notion that a society needs to find ways of allowing as many people as possible to function well within the society, firstly as a philosophical notion of equality but also, perhaps more cynically, as a way of harnessing all available skills for the benefit of a society's economy.

Research into the outcomes for participants in the curriculum show that they are less likely to develop antisocial patterns of behaviour than children who had other types of pre-school experiences. In this context the researchers into the High Scope curriculum also provide a financial rationale for the curriculum. They claim that, in America, for every dollar spent on the curriculum seven dollars are saved. These calculations are based upon an assessment of welfare payments, schooling costs, taxes lost and gained, the cost of criminal justice and victim of crime compensation.

Implementing the High Scope curriculum
The High Scope curriculum has a number of features that clearly identify it:

- room organisation
- equipment organisation
- the daily routine
- the role of the adult.

There is also a series of key terms and concepts that are used in a unique way and combine to form the High Scope curriculum model. They are interdependent and need to be implemented as a complete system involving:
- key experiences
- cognitively orientated programmes
- child-initiated activities
- frameworks
- developmental appropriateness.

Room organisation

In the High Scope curriculum the room is divided into distinct work areas which should include a book area, a home area, a construction area and an art area. Equipment is assigned to one of these areas and the area must be clearly labelled with both pictures and words. The children must be involved in setting up these areas from the outset but the areas are not static and can be changed according to need.

Equipment organisation

All equipment and materials should be accessible to the children at all times without adult intervention. The equipment must be labelled. This can be done in a number of ways, such as with pictures, photographs, silhouettes or words. As with room organisation it is desirable that the children make the decisions about the organisation of the equipment.

The daily routine

The sequence of the day is plan; do; and review. In the planning session the children decide what they are going to do during the session. This is done alongside an adult who encourages elaboration of the plan and, where appropriate, helps the child to record it.

The 'do' session is worktime. Here the children carry out the planned activities. They get their chosen activity out and put it away when they have finished playing with it. Where appropriate this should include craft materials. If their initial plan is finished they make another one. The next phase is 'Clear up time' where the children take responsibility for clearing, sorting, storing in containers and putting away all the materials and equipment used during that session.

The review phase involves the children in describing what they have done during the session, often within a small group. This recall is often accompanied by some form of representation such as drawing, exhibiting their work or verbally describing their play. Recall may be incorporated into 'small group time' when the children are involved in structured, often adult led, activities.

There are also sessions of 'outside time' and 'circle time'. 'Outside time' involves vigorous activity, usually outdoors, accompanied by adult encouragement to talk about the activity. 'Circle time' is when the whole group get together to sing,

SENSORY MOTOR STAGE, 0–2 YEARS

Children gather information predominantly through their senses of sight and touch	Children process information imagistically

Sensory motor stage, 0–2 years

Children have a tendency to be egocentric, seeing the world from their own viewpoint	Children use trial and error as their main tool of discovery.

Children in this age range have a limited language ability, therefore, senses other than hearing are predominant in gathering and processing information. Sight and touch are vital senses in enabling a child to gather the information in his/her environment. This information is then processed as images, similar to, but more sophisticated than, pictures or photographs. This processing system is inflexible and has limited use. For example, how would you store the concept of justice in this way? Children, therefore, need to acquire language. It thus becomes immediately obvious, even at this early stage, that there is an important link between language and intellectual development. It is an interdependent relationship.

PRE-OPERATIONAL STAGE, 2–7 YEARS

Children continue to gather information predominantly through the senses of sight and touch but hearing becomes increasingly important

Initially children's information processing is predominantly imagistic. However, it gradually becomes mediated by thought processes as language develops. These are still basic and very dependent upon immediate perceptions of the environment

Children still have a tendency to be egocentric

Pre-conceptual stage, 2–4 years

Children begin to play symbolically, using one object to represent another, for example a bag as a hat, a doll as a baby	Children believe that everything has a consciousness, for example, teddies have feelings, chairs are naughty

Hearing gradually becomes an important sense for information gathering	Thought processes are increasingly mediated by language as it develops

Children are still dependent upon immediate perceptions of the environment and find abstract thought difficult

Intuitive stage, 5–7 years

Symbolic play continues

Children still have a tendency to be egocentric

As language develops children increasingly use this to gather and process information. Language is a complex system of representation and therefore enables a child to develop more complex ways of gathering and processing information. Again the link between language and intellectual development is shown to be vital in children's learning.

Piaget's two stages of learning and understanding by children 0–7 years

because she smashed five plates.' Her answer was based on how many plates were smashed rather than the motive behind the actions. Again, a young child is shown to be dependent upon visual clues to interpret events. This also demonstrates a young child's inability to use abstract thought to reason (see page 21).

1 What are the implications of the child's perception for their understanding of right and wrong?
2 How may this affect their participation in group games and/or activities?
3 What are the implications for the adult's role?

The development of concepts

Once a child has a reasonable language ability information can be processed as concepts. Concepts are the way in which information is organised. For example, a whole range of meanings can be recalled by the words 'dry', 'high', 'time', 'love' or 'freedom'. Concepts range from basic – wet, long, colour– to those that are more complex and abstract – love, freedom, justice.

Pre-school-aged children are at the stage of developing, adapting and refining basic concepts. Concepts are developed through interaction with the environment in a way that is meaningful to the child. Play provides the opportunity for children to achieve this. For example, initial information about the concept of wet may develop during bathtime when children can feel water on their skin. The concept is further developed by children going out in the rain and seeing and feeling the rain on their skin, clothes and on the ground. The concept is further extended by the children's playing in wet and dry sand.

Piaget describes how children acquire skills and concepts (Piaget uses the term 'schema') through the processes of assimilation and accommodation. Assimilation is the way in which children take in information from their experiences. Accommodation is the way in which children adapt existing information to accommodate new experiences into existing concepts or schemas. The processes of assimilation and accommodation are ongoing and even as adults we are constantly refining existing concepts to accommodate new information.

The diagram on page 23 shows how a child may develop a concept of the physical characteristics of bricks through play. It includes other terms used by Piaget:

- equilibrium – when a child has successfully assimilated and accommodated information into a concept
- disequilibrium – when a child comes across a new experience that requires assimilation or accommodation.

It is clear from this diagram that certain experiences are necessary for children to develop, adapt and refine their concepts:

- a stimulating environment that provides a wide variety of experiences
- the opportunity for repetition of experiences
- the opportunity to extend their learning through differing explorations of similar activities.

Initially these may seem to be conflicting requirements, that a child needs a wide variety of activities but also a significant amount of repetition. Staff need to be aware when activities need changing and when children need to repeat the activity to

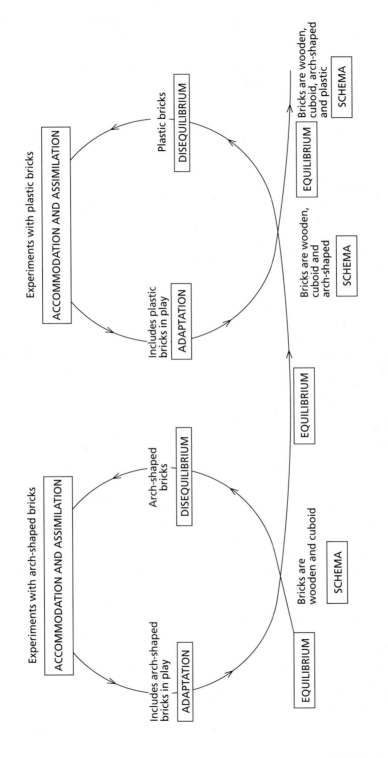

Example of a child developing a schema for bricks using Piaget's terms

consolidate their learning. The curriculum must, therefore, be carefully planned and monitored for this to be achieved. These issues are dealt with in more depth in chapters three and five.

Piaget's work can be seen to provide a rationale for play as an appropriate way for young children to learn. Play allows a child to experience a multi-sensory approach to learning. It provides the opportunity for children to explore the world in a meaningful way to adapt and refine their concepts. Repetition is possible and there is scope for developing more complex concepts through differentiated use of equipment. It is, therefore, developmentally appropriate, so a pre-school curriculum should ensure that play is the medium through which young children are taught.

GOOD PRACTICE

An understanding of Piaget's work has implications for good practice with young children. Clearly, experiential learning, or play, is the best practice in order to meet young children's needs. In addition to this, certain experiences are particularly significant at different stages of development.

Play at the sensory motor stage provides opportunities for:
- using the senses, especially sight and touch while developing language skills
- a wide range of experiences but with plenty of repetition to enable the child to practice and refine skills
- play with other children although the expectation at this stage is that children will play alone.

Play at the pre-operational stage provides opportunities for:
- engaging in symbolic play
- using language during play and to reflect on experiences
- games with simple, straightforward rules
- being alone as well as playing with other children.

Piaget's work has remained important in early-years education until the present day. However, further research work has questioned some of his assumptions. In the 1970s a group led by Margaret Donaldson challenged a number of Piaget's findings. In general they were critical of the way in which Piaget asked questions in experimental situations. They believed that there was a tendency to try and 'catch children out' rather than try to help them. Consequently they contend that if pre-school-aged children are given optimal help in solving a problem then it could be demonstrated that some of Piaget's assumptions about children's cognitive development were incorrect. Donaldson also stressed that pre-school-aged children understand things much better if they are presented in natural settings rather than the artificial setting of a classroom or a laboratory (Sutherland, 1992). There were a number of experiments done to demonstrate their views and to challenge Piaget's conclusions.

The most significant experiment in the context of children's systems of taking in and processing information is the work of Martin Hughes in 1978 (Sutherland, 1992). Piaget said that young children are egocentric, that they were not capable of seeing another person's point of view. Hughes challenged the view. He devised a cross-shaped screen to test this. The child is able to see the policeman and the doll. Hughes found that, after some training, nearly all children between the ages of three

Research has investigated the ways in which both children and adults spend their time during supervised free play sessions. It is important to note that the results outlined below are not a comment on provision but on how the children interacted with the activities and how adults interacted with the children involved in play.

Child behaviour during supervised free play sessions was investigated by several researchers. Tizard et al. in 1976 stated: 'Much play is at a rather low level – brief and simple. This may be because children are distracted by the richness of alternative materials or by the other children present, and are not under pressure from staff to persist with their activity.

Similar research by Sylva et al. in 1980 found: 'There was a lack of challenging activity in children's play. It tended to be brief and involve simple repetitive activities. Sustained conversations were rare.'

Burberry's research in 1980 reported: 'Most of the children's activities were simple and of short duration and there was little adult–child talk, with virtually no sustained conversation.'

Meadows and Cashdan in 1988 stated: 'Within a nursery setting life was pleasant enough for most children. Fights, quarrels and upsets were rare, but so were discovery, achievement after endeavour and intellectual challenge. Some play bouts were brief, others went on interminably at the same repetitive activity. Some children remained on the margins of activity, drifting unengaged from one activity to another without ever sustaining either conversation or involvement with task or material. Though the classroom norm was happy, enough children fell below an acceptable level, and few achieved their potential in terms of creativity, cooperation and challenge, that the free play curriculum could not be said to be meeting children's needs.'

Staff behaviour during supervised free play sessions was also investigated by Tizard and Phillips in 1976, who noted how adults' time was spent during free play sessions:

- 50 per cent, talking to children, in management and in conversation
- 46 per cent supervising and dealing with equipment
- 4 per cent playing with children.

Clift, in 1980, noted the average times adults spent with the children during sessions:

- involvement in a child's activity, 98 seconds
- conversation with a child, 35 seconds
- working with children, 52 seconds.

The research showed that staff changed task on average 175 times in $2\frac{1}{2}$ hours. That is equal to 70 tasks per hour.

Current research confirms these findings and extends our understanding of the best provision for pre-school-aged children. Nabuco and Sylva, in 1995, researched the comparative effects of three different curricula which differed in the amount of free choice and guided choice within them. It was found that children who had participated in a curriculum that included a balance of free and guided choices benefited most from their pre-school experiences. Significantly, the findings demonstrated benefits across the whole of the curriculum:

- higher academic skills in reading and writing

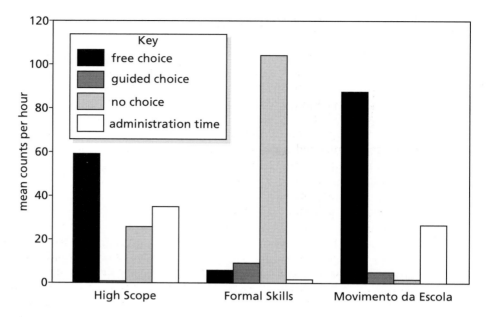

A balanced combination of free and guided choices is most beneficial for pre-school-aged children (Nabuco and Sylva, 1995)

- a high level of pretend play
- a high level of informal conversation
- a low level of anxiety on entering school
- a positive effect on children's perception of their own social acceptance and competence.

Other research further demonstrated the benefits of a structured curriculum on children's social and emotional skills. Paley, in 1992, shows how an adult encourages cooperation among pre-school-aged children (Sylva, 1995). The rule 'you can't say you can't play' was introduced through a combination of storytelling and group discussion. The rule was maintained through storytelling and the use of puppets. The outcome was a transformation in tolerance and cooperation within the group. This is an excellent example of adult guidance towards a desired outcome using the children's level and means of understanding as a starting point.

The learning framework within a pre-school setting must therefore acknowledge the importance of adult and child interaction in the learning process. Children in pre-school settings are in a group situation where the adult to child ratio is much higher than in a family setting. A smaller adult to child ratio allows for a higher level of adult and child interaction. In a group setting, therefore, planning needs to take account of this and provide the time and opportunity for a high level of interaction to take place. There are clearly management issues involved in developing a curriculum that allows for a high level of adult and child interaction and these are covered in chapter three.

Maintaining a child-centred approach

A framework for learning is provided by an adult who provides the play environment, interacts with the child when appropriate directing the play through questioning, suggestion, demonstration and encouragement and monitors and assesses both the children and the activity to inform future planning. If the learning experiences provided are to be genuinely child-centred the adults need to establish a number of things about each child to ensure that the way in which the learning experiences are planned and delivered is appropriate to the children in the group.

■ What is the child interested in?
■ What skills does the child bring to the nursery?
■ What is the child good at?
■ How does this link with the curriculum?

These starting points provide a focus for the development of learning experiences that are meaningful to each individual child. It is important that the curriculum should develop from a blend of the children's abilities and interests and the intended outcomes. In this way the curriculum can be differentiated to meet the individual needs of the children within the setting. This is fundamental to good practice with children. All children have different experiences, interests, skills and levels of ability, and these need to be established and incorporated into curriculum planning.

It is, of course, of equal importance to develop a relaxed ethos that allows for informal adult and child interaction alongside this more structured approach. As Sylva's research shows, a combination of free and guided play is most beneficial to a pre-school-aged child.

CASE STUDY

Using a child's interests as a starting point for learning

Ranjit, a three-year-old, developed an interest in the guinea pigs in the nursery. He spent a lot of time watching their movements. He brought in food for them and was keen to clean their cage out. An adult noticed his interest. Initially she joined the child while he was watching the guinea pigs and asked the child to describe what he saw. They talked about what the guinea pigs looked like, what they ate, how important it was to feed and look after them and about their daily pattern of eating and sleeping.

At storytime the adult encouraged the child to tell the other children what they had observed together. They used a book about guinea pigs to illustrate what they were saying.

The adult had used the child's interest as her starting point in developing the child's learning. In her interaction with him she had begun to develop a number of the child's skills:

■ exploration and recognition of living things
■ events and patterns in the natural world
■ powers of observation
■ recognition of appropriate treatment of living things

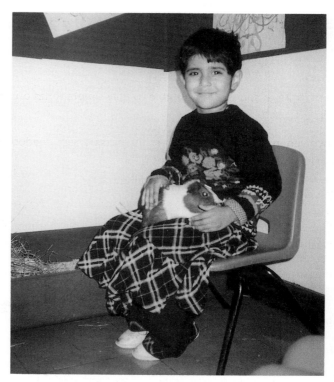

Children's own interests are a good starting point for their learning

- demonstration of feeling towards experiences of the world
- use of language to express thoughts and convey meaning
- knowledge that words and pictures carry meaning
- one of the purposes of writing i.e. to record information
- development of confidence and self esteem.

1 Why was the child's interest in the guinea pigs a good starting point for the child's learning?
2 Identify how the different skills were developed.
3 How could the adult further extend this child's learning?

Once each individual child's interests and abilities have been established, learning experiences can be planned taking these into account. This involves careful assessment and record keeping involving both parents/carers and pre-school staff. The initial profile of each child should be established early on in their time at the pre-school setting usually alongside parents/carers. These initial and ongoing evaluations of children should be reflected in long, medium and short term planning. The curriculum needs to be flexible enough to differentiate each child's learning in accordance with their individual profile.

A differentiated curriculum

From the baseline assessment done alongside parents/carers it was evident that Sam and her family had musical ability. Sam sang well and had a wide repertoire of songs. She was able to play simple tunes on a recorder, was familiar with a wide range of musical instruments and was learning to play the piano and the viola. The staff were aware that as well as being involved in the music activities in the nursery Sam needed other experiences to broaden and develop her skills.

The differentiated nursery curriculum enabled Sam to broaden her experience of songs, instruments and music from other cultures. The staff encouraged Sam to teach the other children songs that she knew and to learn songs from them. These experiences were extended by involving Sam in workshops provided by local professional musicians.

The nursery curriculum can broaden children's experience with songs, instruments and music from other cultures

1 What was the starting point for the staff and how did they establish this?
2 How were Sam's needs met?
3 Suggest other ways in which Sam's needs could be met.

GOOD PRACTICE

Positive adult and child interaction is necessary for young children's learning. A combination of free and guided play is of most benefit to pre-school children's learning. The adult's role in the learning is predominantly one of facilitator, although it is acknowledged that sometimes it is necessary to give children information.

The starting point for pre-school children's learning must be the child's abilities and interests linked to the curriculum content. This will ensure that the curriculum provided is meaningful to individual children.

PROGRESS CHECK

1 What is free play?

2 What questions can be raised about the suitability of free play for children's learning?

3 What are Bussis' four dimensions of learning?

4 Why is 'open education' most suitable for young children?

5 Read through again the research evidence on children's play. What conclusions can be drawn?

Creating a positive learning framework

There needs be a clear idea of the required outcomes on which learning experiences can be based. This is provided by the curriculum outline which is covered in detail in chapters five to nine. Planning needs to take account of the curriculum outline, the children's abilities and a range of practical considerations such as staffing, accommodation and other resources. This is covered in detail in chapter four.

Providing a stimulating environment is an important starting point. The activities provided must be developmentally appropriate and flexible enough to allow for individual needs. Provision must take account of each child's need for a variety of experiences and repetition that enables consolidation of skills and concepts.

Positive and meaningful interaction during children's play needs a focus. Vygotsky describes this as 'a zone of proximal development' suggesting that a child

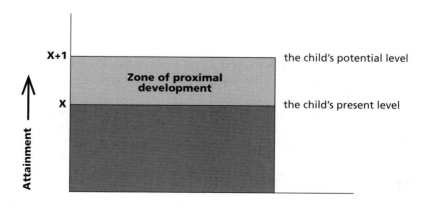

Vygotsky's zone of proximal development

has two stages of development: their present one; and the next step that can, as yet, only be achieved with adult help. The adult needs to support the child's learning until the child can achieve the next step alone. As childcare workers it is essential to be aware of both stages of development so each individual child's needs can be met.

Jerome Bruner describes this process as 'scaffolding' a child's learning. This is an analogy of the scaffolding put up around a building to support it while it is being built. Once the building is complete the scaffolding can be removed and the building stand alone. Similarly, the adult's role is to put a scaffold around the child's learning to support it until the child can achieve the learning to operate independently at that level.

Janet Moyles (1989) develops this concept in her play spiral (see page 36). She stresses the importance of children being allowed free play in between structured play sessions to enable them to consolidate their learning. This pattern allows both an interactive and experiential curriculum to be developed to meet the children's needs.

The first session of free play allowed exploration, the second allowed a degree of mastery. The directed play by the teacher channelled the exploration and learning from the free play and took the children a stage further forward from where they then were in terms of understanding. Rather like a pebble on a pond, the ripples from the exploratory free play extended through directed play and back to enhance and enrich free play, allowed a spiral of learning spreading ever outwards into wider experiences for the children and upwards into the accretion of knowledge and skills.

(Just Playing, *J. Moyles, 1989*)

CASE STUDY

The play spiral

A new theme of a clinic was set up in the role play area. It was introduced to small groups of children at a time. The staff discussed with the children what had been provided and introduced new vocabulary. At storytime the books chosen introduced play themes that the children may have liked to follow. All the children were initially allowed free play in the area.

A member of staff focused on Amy with special educational needs that had resulted in her expressive language being delayed. The adult observed the play themes that were emerging in the child's free play and joined in the play as a patient coming to the clinic. While playing, the adult encouraged Amy to use language for a variety of means: to describe, to discuss, to direct and to imagine.

Further free play followed when the adult, once again, observed Amy to enable her to join in the play and encourage the development of the child's expressive language.

The pattern, outlined in the Moyles spiral, of free and directed play sequences, was implemented by taking account of the individual child's needs, interests and abilities.

1 Identify where and how the child was able to engage in experiential and interactive play.
2 How did the experiential and interactive play complement each other?
3 How could the adult extend and develop this child's learning through play?

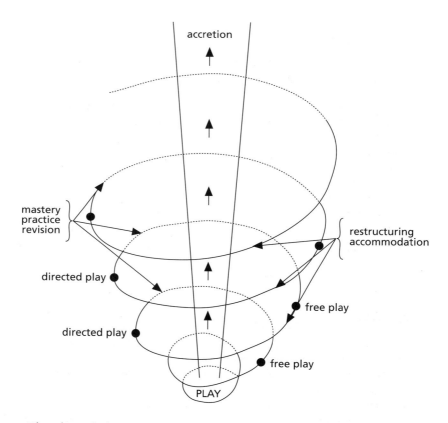

The play spiral

PROGRESS CHECK

1 What does positive and meaningful interaction depend upon?
2 What is Vygotsky's zone of proximal development?
3 What does Bruner mean by 'scaffolding'?

4 What are the implications of Vygotsky's and Bruner's work for childcare workers?

5 Describe Moyles' play spiral.

6 What are the implications of the play spiral for good practice?

We can conclude that the following important points must be the focus of all practice in the pre-school environment.

- Play is the most appropriate learning medium for pre-school-aged children.
- Adult–child interaction is necessary to children's learning.
- A combination of free and guided choices is the most beneficial to a child's learning.

KEY TERMS

You need to know what these words and phrases mean. Go back through the chapter and make sure that you understand:

accommodation	experiential learning
assimilation	facilitator
child-centred	free play
concept	guided play
concrete experiences	interactive
developmentally appropriate	play spiral
differentiated	pre-operational stage
directed play	scaffolding
disequilibrium	sensory motor stage
equilibrium	zone of proximal development
ethos	

Further reading

Bruce, T., *Early Childhood Education,* Hodder & Stoughton, 1987

Manning, K. and Sharp, A., *Structuring Play in the Early Years at School,* Ward Locke, 1977

Meadows, S. and Cashdan, A., *Helping Children Learn,* David Fulton, 1988

Moyles, J., *Just Playing: The role and status of play in early childhood education,* Open University Press, 1989

Sutherland, P., *Cognitive Development Today, Piaget and His Critics,* Paul Chapman Press, 1992

Whitehead, M., *Language and Literacy in the Early Years,* Paul Chapman Press, 1990

3 ASPECTS OF GOOD PRACTICE

Equal opportunities and the individuality of the child

When we plan the curriculum we need to bear in mind the differences between children as well as their similarities. Within any group of three- to five-year-olds there will be wide variations in development and maturity alongside differences in their social, cultural, religious and racial backgrounds. For children to fulfil their potential, pre-school staff need to take account of this and provide a curriculum that meets the social, emotional, physical and intellectual needs of each individual child in their care. This is a challenging task and responding by treating all children in exactly the same way will not provide for equal opportunities for all.

We must recognise the ways in which children experience disadvantage and be responsible for presenting the curriculum in a way that includes and enables all children and that reflects all sections of society. The planning and delivery of the curriculum can promote equal opportunities irrespective of race and culture, gender, socio-economic background or disability. It must also consider how best to develop the potential of children who are more timid or aggressive or more confident than might be expected of the group. A child-centred approach to the curriculum will recognise and respond to each child's individuality. The following case study raises some of these issues.

CASE STUDY

Responding to individuality
Tasneem, William and Marcia, all aged just three, had started nursery at the same time, six weeks earlier. Tasneem was the youngest child in the family and her three brothers and sisters had all attended the nursery. Tasneem had grown up in an extended family setting and was confident, lively and outgoing. The presence of her slightly older cousin in the nursery helped her to settle into the routine fairly quickly. At home Tasneem's family conversations were usually in Punjabi, but English was spoken too.

Tasneem could speak and understand English but at nursery she appeared unwilling to do so. At 'carpet time' she listened intently to the songs and rhymes but had yet to join in.

William was an only child and had spent a lot of time in adult company. His speech was well-developed as were his self-care skills. At nursery he was quiet and watchful, hovering around the edge of activities and not joining in with the group. He spent a great deal of time in the book corner where he was often alone. He seemed wary of the older, more boisterous children and sought out the adults in the nursery.

Marcia's family had just moved to the area. Her mother had just had a baby and was finding it hard to cope. Marcia took some time to settle at nursery and found it difficult to let her mother leave. During the session she tended to move from one activity to another, never really exploring what she could do, often pushing and shoving other children. Her spoken language was quite limited and the children found her hard to understand.

The nursery staff had been observing the children during the settling-in period and felt that all three had particular needs to be met before the children could gain most from their nursery experience.

1 Look at each child individually. What do you see as their needs?
2 What could the staff do to meet these needs?

The pre-school curriculum transmits not just skills and knowledge but attitudes and values too. These early years are crucial in the formation of children's attitudes about themselves and about the world they live in. A curriculum that promotes equality of opportunity will enable children to feel positively about themselves and their achievements, to avoid the limitations of stereotyping and to value diversity. Pre-school workers also play a significant part in shaping children's attitudes and should be aware of their influence as role models.

GOOD PRACTICE

Children will derive most benefit from their pre-school experience if they are accepted and valued for who they are. The Children Act 1989 requires that needs arising from children's race, culture, religion and language be considered by those caring for them.

DO EQUAL OPPORTUNITIES MATTER AT THIS AGE?

There is a belief that young children do not notice skin colour and that this is not an issue for the pre-school years. Research by Milner in 1983 and Maximé in 1986 has challenged this, demonstrating that black and white children as young as three attach value to skin colour, perceiving white skin as 'better' than black. This indicates that children absorb messages about racial stereotyping from a very early age. These can be very damaging to black children and affect their self-esteem. Harm is done to white children too unless this perception of racial superiority is confronted and challenged effectively. Such findings underline the need for all-white settings to recognise this and to provide for an approach that challenges this stereotyping.

Research by Browne and France, in 1986, into the influence that gender stereotyping has on children's play shows that pre-school children often have strong ideas about what girls and boys can do. Observations in this study demonstrated that some types of play were dominated by one sex and that all of the children did not participate in all of the activities because some were perceived to be 'for girls' or 'for boys'. This can result in boys and girls having a very limited view of the choices available to males and females in our society.

Ensure that boys and girls can participate fully in all activities on offer

Children with special needs benefit greatly from pre-school learning opportunities which encourage them to fulfil their potential. Pre-school provision for children with special needs may be in special centres but most mainstream units include children with special needs among their numbers. The challenge for the centre here is for staff to assess the child's needs and use their professional expertise to meet these, differentiating the curriculum where necessary. Self-esteem will flourish in a setting where children are welcomed and valued for themselves, not in situations where the child's development is hindered through limited opportunities and low expectations.

CASE STUDY

Providing for special needs

Rahila had been blind since birth. Her parents were offered a playgroup place for her at a school for visually impaired children when she was three but they chose to send her to the nursery class of the local school which both her sisters had attended. At first the staff were apprehensive and concerned that the nursery might not be able to provide a suitable environment for a blind child, but after discussing these concerns with the parents, they agreed that she should attend. The staff spent some time looking at the physical environment and identifying pathways around the nursery that could be indicated with tactile markers for Rahila to follow. They planned activities ensuring that no child, including Rahila, would be excluded from participating.

Rahila made visits to the nursery with her parents prior to starting. The other children were initially curious and asked questions about blindness which were answered in a straightforward way. She settled quickly and confidently into the nursery participating fully in all the activities, sometimes with adult assistance, more often independently. Sometimes children would try to do tasks for her rather than let her do things for herself but the staff and Rahila herself made sure that this didn't happen. Equipment and advice were available to the nursery from the local visually impaired unit and from the Royal National Institute for the Blind. Rahila transferred to school at five, competent and confident and having benefited greatly from her pre-school experience.

1 What made Rahila's experience so successful?
2 What is the adults' role here?
3 Which agencies could give help and advice to staff supporting children with disabilities?

PROVIDING FOR EQUAL OPPORTUNITIES

Providing for equal opportunities is a complex process that requires staff to look critically at their own attitudes, values and behaviour as well as the activities and resources they offer. For maximum benefit to the children the following need to be considered.

- Staff commitment and a recognition of the importance of an equal opportunities approach.
- Seeing equal opportunities as an integral part of any curriculum and not as an optional add-on in particular situations.
- Looking at the learning environment and resources and evaluating the way that they are used.
- A willingness to seek out advice and ideas and to learn from others.
- Communicating with parents, explaining your approach and responding when challenged.
- Keeping equal opportunities on the agenda through the process of monitoring and evaluation.

CASE STUDY

Promoting cultural diversity
The under-eights' officer who was responsible for registering and inspecting playgroups in a rural area was concerned that the playgroups'

resources lacked any representation of cultural diversity. At a meeting with some of the playgroup workers she raised this as an issue. Some responded by saying that they felt that this was an issue for the inner city but not for them. Others recognised this gap in their provision and cited lack of funds and lack of knowledge. After some discussion the group decided on a way forward. The under-eight's officer organised a series of evening meetings open to all playgroup workers in the area and speakers from the library service, educational suppliers and resource centres were invited. The group discussions that followed examined the benefits to all children of positive images and the implications of the 'invisibility' of some groups. On subsequent visits to the playgroups the under-eight's officer noticed changes in the displays and the resources on offer and in particular the range of books borrowed from the local library.

1 How could the playgroup workers develop this initiative to promote cultural diversity further?

2 What are the benefits of introducing a culturally diverse curriculum in an all-white setting?

The following section suggests some practical pointers towards promoting equal opportunities through the curriculum.

In the visual environment

■ Display positive images in the setting. Black people, women and people with disabilities are under-represented in the wider visual environment. Choose images that challenge stereotypes, such as a black barrister, a disabled doctor, or a woman police officer.

Give children the opportunity to represent themselves accurately

- Give children the opportunity to represent themselves accurately. Provide mirrors and paints and crayons that enable children to match their own skin tones.
- Look at the illustrations in books and posters that you provide. Do they convey a positive image or do you see line drawings of white children shaded to represent black, girls always in the background taking a supporting role, disabled people as helpless and reliant on others.
- Visitors in the setting can challenge stereotypes, perhaps a father with his new baby, a black dentist or a female electrician.

Visitors to the centre can challenge stereotypes

Choosing toys and planning activities
- Look at jigsaws, games, play figures, musical instruments and their packaging too. Do they reflect cultural diversity? Do they encourage both boys and girls to play? Are children with disabilities represented?
- Provide dolls that represent different racial groups with appropriate clothes. Do not buy black dolls that have white facial features or hair. Monitor the way that the dolls are played with. Think of the message conveyed when the white dolls are tucked up in prams and the black dolls thrown into a box. Encourage boys to show that they can cuddle and care for 'babies'.
- Home corner play can be a secure and comforting play space. Make sure that your provision of cooking equipment and play food reflects a variety of cultural preferences. If you introduce some new or unfamiliar equipment such as chopsticks, for example, make sure that the children know how to use it properly.
- Dressing-up clothes give children an opportunity to elaborate their role play. Avoid identifying items as 'for boys' or 'for girls' and encourage children to try out everything. Provide everyday clothes from a range of cultures but do not over generalise – Pakistani children are as likely to wear tracksuits or jeans as they are shalwar-kameez!

- Celebrate a range of festivals. Children who celebrate these festivals at home will feel valued and others can gain an insight and understanding. Care needs to be taken in this area to avoid a tokenistic approach with an emphasis on the 'exotic' aspects of cultural differences. Festival celebrations need to be researched carefully if they are to have any real educational significance. Enlist help from community groups or parents. (Think about the message that you are sending about the relative worth of festivals if you spend six weeks building up to Christmas and an afternoon on Diwali.)

Celebrate a range of festivals

- Cooking sessions can present an opportunity to try different recipes and taste a range of foods. It can also provide children with a chance to confront any stereotypical ideas about whose job it is to cook. Again, when talking about cultural preferences in diet avoid over-generalisations. Children from Caribbean families may like to eat rice and peas but they will also eat pizza and visit McDonalds.
- Make sure that activities are not dominated by one group of children to the exclusion of others. It may be necessary to exclude one group for a while so that others can have a chance to gain confidence and skills.
- Provision for creative activities should reflect cultural diversity. Introduce children to a range of artistic traditions and styles and provide a range of materials for them to work with. Play all kinds of music and provide instruments and this will influence the children's own music-making.
- Make sure that all children can participate in the range of activities, including those with disabilities. This may involve an adjustment to the physical environment such as moving a construction activity to a table-top so that a child in a wheelchair can reach it or it may mean providing appropriate equipment such as

tactile dominoes so that a child with a visual impairment can be included in the game.

Resources cannot in themselves promote equal opportunities. It is up to staff to understand the principles behind carefully chosen resources and activities and to present them in ways that develop awareness.

Recognising the power of language

- Value language diversity. Encourage children to listen to languages other than their own. Teach greetings and rhymes and share dual-language books with children.
- Choose books and tell stories that challenge stereotypes and provide positive role models.
- Introduce stories and rhymes from many literary traditions.
- Language is a powerful influence in shaping children's self-esteem and identity. Be aware of the words that you use. Avoid terms that associate black with negative connotations e.g. black mood, accident black spot, black magic rather than descriptively – black paint, black coffee, black trousers. Sexist comments about 'strong boys' and 'pretty girls' reinforce stereotypes. Challenge abusive words such as 'cripple', 'mongol', 'spastic' when you hear them used by adults and by children.

Interacting with children and with adults

- Let children know that you value them for themselves. Start by considering their individual personalities and build on their individual experiences.
- Ensure that all children benefit from interaction with adults. Some children insist on your attention. Make sure that the quieter, less demanding children are also noticed.
- Take seriously any incidence of name-calling or bullying. It is not enough to comfort the victim; the behaviour must be challenged and be seen to be unacceptable.
- Be prepared to explain your approach to parents. They are more likely to share your aims and values if they know what they are and the reasons for them.
- Take positive action. If you notice that one child or group of children is at a disadvantage, intervene and find another approach.
- Question your own attitudes and values. Do you accept rough play more readily from boys than from girls? Do you have low expectations of children from some socio-economic groups, of children from ethnic minority groups or of children with disabilities?
- Make an equal opportunities perspective integral to your curriculum planning and evaluate your achievements.

Pre-school workers are very influential in the formation of children's attitudes and values. Children will take their cue from adult responses and reactions and it is therefore important that staff do not skate over issues of equality.

PROGRESS CHECK

1 Why is it important to consider the individuality of each child when planning the curriculum?

2 Why are equal opportunities an important aspect of the pre-school curriculum?

3 How can equal opportunities be promoted through the curriculum?

4 What is stereotyping and why should we challenge stereotypes?

5 Is the issue of equal opportunities an issue for all settings? Why?

6 Why should childcare staff question their own attitudes and values?

Special Educational Needs and the Code of Practice

The Code of Practice for Special Educational Needs was introduced as part of the measures required under the Education Act 1993 and all maintained schools are required to adopt it. It provides a framework for the identification and assessment of children with special education needs (SEN) and aims to tackle the following issues:
- inconsistencies in the way resources are allocated
- the length of time taken to assess children and make appropriate provision
- the lack of information given to parents
- the lack of weight often given to parents' wishes.
    The code emphasises:
- early action
- close collaboration between agencies
- the partnership between centres and parents and children.

    Any centre receiving government funding for pre-school education will be required to adopt the Code of Practice, devising their own special needs policy in the light of these requirements. Normally a special needs coordinator (SENCO) will be appointed who will take responsibility for the day-to-day operation of the policy which will include maintaining a register and records of children identified as having a special educational need and advising and liaising with colleagues, with parents and with other agencies who may be involved with the child. Information about the operation of the Code of Practice and the Special Needs policy should be published in the centre's handbook and be available to parents.

THE FIVE STAGES OF ASSESSMENT

The process leading up to statutory assessment and statementing can be tracked through five stages, from stage 1 – initial identification of a special need – through to stage 5 – statementing. The Code envisages that the needs of most children will be met through steps taken at stages 1, 2 and 3 and that only very few children will meet the criteria for statutory assessment and statementing.

Stage 1
- Observation and information gathering contribute to the initial identification of

the child's special educational need. Information may also be available on admission as part of a referral from the GP, health visitor or social worker.

- Parents are consulted, the head of the centre informed and the child is entered on the register.
- Specialist help may be sought and it is likely that the curriculum will be differentiated in some ways.
- Records must be kept that document the process and set a date for a review of progress that must be within six months. If progress is not satisfactory with these measures after two reviews, then the process moves to stage 2.

Stage 2

The SEN coordinator gathers together all information from stage 1. Further advice may be sought and parents are again consulted. An Individual Education Plan (IEP) may be created at this stage. This will set out the following.

- The nature of the child's learning difficulties.
- Action to be taken, including staffing needs, resources and any special programmes.
- Targets to be achieved within a given time.
- Any necessary medical arrangements.
- Arrangements for monitoring and assessing progress.
- Arrangements for review.

If the review at stage 2 indicates that more steps need to be taken to support progress, then stage 3 will be implemented.

Stage 3

- Responsibility will be shared with other professionals such as visiting specialists or educational psychologists.
- A new IEP, as above, will be drawn up indicating new strategies and targets and detailing specific support for the child.
- If the review favours moving towards statutory assessment, then all relevant information will be gathered together.

Stage 4 Statutory Assessment

- Statutory assessment is the responsibility of the LEA. The process should be completed within 26 weeks.
- Centres will need to provide documentary evidence that despite the steps taken through stages 1 to 3, the child's needs remain so great that they cannot be provided from resources 'ordinarily available'.
- Statutory assessment will consider the child's emotional and social needs as well as academic progress.

Stage 5 Statementing

- Statutory assessment will result in a statement that will indicate the child's particular needs and how the LEA will meet those needs with support which may be in mainstream or special provision.
- The statement will often provide access to extra educational resources.

- The statement must show how parental preferences are taken into account.
- The statement will also indicate arrangements for subsequent review.

By no means all children will follow the whole process through. If the review determines that their needs are being met by the centre's approach, then they will stay at that particular stage of support. In some cases the review will determine that they are no longer in need of special provision and they will be taken off the register.

CASE STUDY

Devising an Individual Education Plan

Carla, at three and a half, was taking a very long time to settle into nursery. She spent much of her time drifting from one activity to another without ever really becoming involved. She found it very difficult to form relationships with other children and was often aggressive towards them and disrupted their play. She seemed unable to concentrate at storytime and 'carpet time' but enjoyed looking at books either alone or with a member of staff. The nursery teacher, who also had the responsibility for special needs within the establishment, shared these concerns with Carla's parents. She was included on the SEN register at stage 1 of the assessment process with some differentiation of the curriculum recommended and a review of her progress set for four months.

During this time staff observed Carla closely, particularly her key worker who had most to do with her. Her aggressive behaviour continued and at the review there were still causes for concern. A decision was made to proceed to stage 2 of assessment where an IEP would be devised to meet Carla's needs. The plan set out specific targets for Carla to achieve alongside strategies that would be used to help her. These included some individual time with her key worker each day where concentration and sustaining interest in an activity would be emphasised. The key worker would also work towards integrating Carla into the rest of the group. Her negative, aggressive behaviour would not be tolerated but the emphasis of the plan was on rewarding her achievements. Her parents were fully involved in the plan and were asked to use the same strategies at home and to share their own views on how Carla was progressing with the nursery staff.

After six months, instances of difficult behaviour were less common and the plan was modified slightly to encourage Carla to become more independent of her key worker. Around this time it was discovered that Carla had some degree of hearing loss which might explain some of her difficulties, in particular with storytimes, and would have implications for her new IEP.

1 Why were staff concerned about Carla?
2 How could the SEN Code of Practice help Carla?
3 What should be considered when drawing up an IEP?

In exceptional cases, children will be referred for statutory assessment without proceeding through the early stages as it will be clear from the outset that their needs are significant and substantial. This would include children with a major sensory or physical impairment.

IMPLICATIONS FOR STAFF

The Code of Practice requires centres to identify and assess children's special educational needs and to take action that will support children and enable them to achieve their potential within the educational setting. Pre-school workers will need to observe children closely, formulate plans and targets and differentiate provision appropriately. At every stage of the process parents should be involved and their views taken into account.

PROGRESS CHECK

1 What are the main features of the SEN Code of Practice?
2 How can Individual Education Plans help children with special educational needs?
3 What does a Statement of Special Educational Needs ensure?
4 How does your workplace cater for special educational needs?

Working in partnership with parents

All those who work with young children will recognise that the relationship between the pre-school establishment and parents is a crucial one.

WHY WORK WITH PARENTS?

- Parents have the most knowledge and understanding of their children. Sharing this knowledge with staff enables the staff to build on previous experience in planning for the child's future development.
- Research by Osborn and Milbank in 1987, and others, has demonstrated conclusively the positive effect that parental involvement in the education process has on the progress of children. If parents become involved early on in the child's education they are likely to maintain this involvement, with many benefits to the child, throughout his/her educational career.
- Recent legislation contained within the Education Reform Act 1988, the Children Act 1989 and the Special Educational Needs Code of Practice 1993 places a legal responsibility on those caring for children to work in partnership with parents. Initiatives such as the Parents' Charter emphasise the parents' right to be consulted in decisions concerning their children's education.
- Children are more likely to feel secure and settled if it is clear that there are good channels of communication between parents and staff.
- Children's learning is not confined to the pre-school setting. An exchange of information from centre to home and from home to centre will consolidate learning, wherever it takes place.

- Parents have a wealth of expertise that they can contribute to the pre-school setting. This can broaden and enrich the experience of all children.
- Parents may feel a loss of role when their child starts at a centre. Involvement in the process could help them to adjust to this change.
- Sharing concerns with staff may help parents towards facing and resolving any difficulties they might be experiencing with a child.

GOOD PRACTICE

A meaningful exchange of information between parents and staff is vital to the well-being of the child. Remember that parents may feel uneasy in an unfamiliar setting and it is up to staff to make them feel comfortable and valued.

ESTABLISHING GOOD RELATIONSHIPS

The choices parents make about their child's pre-school education will be dependent on a variety of factors considered alongside their own particular circumstances and needs. Most parents will want to visit the centre before applying for a place and may also talk to parents of children already attending and perhaps consult reports. First impressions do count and lay the foundation for any subsequent relationship.The following may contribute to establishing positive relationships.
- Make parents feel welcome, particularly when they visit for the first time. Meeting parents with a smile and a 'hello' shows that you welcome them. Try to greet parents by name.

Spending time with parents will convey the message that they are welcome in the centre

- Arrange for someone to show prospective parents around and to answer any questions or concerns.
- Try to be flexible when organising talks and visits for new parents. Some parents may have work or family commitments that are difficult to move. A video of the centre in action might be useful if parents are unable to visit during session time and versions can be provided with a commentary in different languages.
- Think about the physical environment. Is the entrance to the centre inviting? Can visitors find the way in? Do displays communicate the philosophy of the centre?
- Most centres provide a brochure. Make sure that yours is clear, concise, current and has a welcoming tone. Provide the brochures in different languages when necessary.
- Make time to talk with parents at some length before the child starts. This will provide an opportunity to exchange information, to answer questions in more detail and to reassure if there are any anxieties. Some centres offer home visits and this may be helpful if parents find it difficult to get out. Also, some parents feel more comfortable if the interview is in their own home.
- Encourage parents to be part of the settling-in process and explain how this is managed in your centre. This can be a difficult time for parents. Do not dismiss worries as trivial and insignificant but reassure wherever possible.

CASE STUDY

Choosing a nursery

Linda took a career break from her job when Marcus was born. She decided to return to work full-time just after his third birthday. There was a number of private day nurseries that would have been convenient between her home and workplace. Lots of her friends had their children cared for at local nurseries and after listening to what they had to say she visited three before making up her mind. When she telephoned the nursery that she eventually chose, she was encouraged to come at a time when the senior nursery nurse would be free to take her around and to bring Marcus with her.

The main door opened into a bright entrance hall where children's work was displayed around a notice board that carried information about the nursery and other reminders to parents. Linda was met by Sonia, the senior nursery nurse, who greeted her and Marcus by name and then took them on a tour of the nursery, explaining the organisation of the rooms and the staffing. Linda had plenty of questions which Sonia answered readily. Both Marcus and Linda were introduced to staff including the nursery nurse whose home group he would be in. Over a cup of tea, Linda explained that Marcus had eczema and needed some special care. She also wanted to know whether the nursery could provide vegetarian food as this was the family's preference. Sonia was able to respond to these concerns and noted them down. As Linda and Marcus were leaving, Sonia gave Linda a copy of the nursery brochure and told her that she should get in touch if she had any questions or concerns

Linda went home impressed by what she had seen and Marcus was very happy to talk about what he would be doing at 'his' nursery. Marcus started at the nursery two weeks before Linda returned to work, attending for a couple of hours a day to begin with and building up to the full day that he needed to get used to. Throughout this time Linda was encouraged to spend time in the nursery with Marcus, gradually taking more and more time out of the room as Marcus settled into the routine. She found that this time in the nursery gave her a clearer understanding of their philosophy and practice. When she started back to work full-time she knew that she could telephone the nursery if she had any concerns about Marcus.

1 What do you think made Linda choose this nursery?
2 Brochures can be very comprehensive. Can they be a substitute for face-to-face contact?
3 Linda had some particular points that she wanted to raise with Sonia. Think of other areas of concern for parents.

WORKING TOGETHER

Good relationships established around the entry and the settling-in period should be used to promote the ongoing exchange of information between parents and staff. Centres need to appreciate that parents will want to know if their children are settled and happy, how they are progressing, what they are doing and how they can support their children's learning.

Personal information

Staff and parents need to exchange information about individual children on a regular basis. Events in a child's life such as a new baby, illness in the family, a parent working away from home or different medication may all affect behaviour in the pre-school setting. If staff are aware of this they are better able to respond to the child's needs. Parents and staff also need opportunities to raise concerns and decide on a way forward. This kind of one-to-one exchange of information depends on staff making time for parents and on parents having confidence in the individual members of staff concerned.

CASE STUDY

Expressing concerns

Miranda had been coming happily to nursery for over a year. She was lively and interested, taking a full part in everything that was on offer. Recently she had been tearful at leaving her mother at the beginning of the session and reluctant to join in with the activities, spending most of her time on the cushions in the reading corner. At home time the nursery nurse responsible for the group made a point of having a word with Miranda's mother about her concerns and asked if she could think of what might have upset her. She said that Miranda's father had recently had to take a job away from home and that they were all having some difficulty adjusting to this new pattern of family life.

1 How can the nursery help Miranda through this difficult period?
2 What provision do you make in your setting for parents to share this kind of individual information?

Progress and achievements

Parents will want to know how their child is progressing and be able to mark and support achievements. Centres will vary in the ways that they communicate this information to parents but individual records should be kept and shared with parents regularly. Many centres run parents' afternoons or evenings when staff talk with parents individually. Others use diary-type booklets that are regularly written up and sent home with the children for parents to read and make comments in. Information about a child's progress can also be passed on in less formal ways when parents collect children – 'he worked hard on that painting', 'she pedalled the tricycle all around the playground'. Parents should also be encouraged to contribute to the record-keeping process linking their own observations to those of the staff thus emphasising the role that the home plays in children's learning.

Explaining the curriculum

The centre's brochure will probably give a general indication of curriculum aims and methods to parents. More detailed information can be gained in a number of ways. Some centres display planning for the current topic or theme so that parents know what children will be doing and perhaps become involved themselves by supporting outings or supplying materials. Staff should be prepared to discuss what they are doing with parents and be able to explain and justify their methods. Open evenings where staff explain and demonstrate their approach can be very helpful in giving parents a clearer picture of what their aims are. Sessions where the centre is set up and parents are encouraged to play and perhaps then evaluate what they have learned are often very successful. Another way of going about this might be to display cards or posters alongside activities indicating what skills and concepts the children might gain from them. Individual pamphlets that explain the centre's approach to, say, reading or maths can be very informative and give parents confidence in their own contributions to their children's learning.

Participating in the curriculum

Parents may be able to contribute to the curriculum in a variety of ways, perhaps by talking to children about their job, by telling a story in another language or by bringing in special materials or equipment. They might also volunteer to accompany groups of children on outings or work alongside children at activities, providing valuable extra adult input. Where parents contribute in these ways, it is important that staff take responsibility for making sure that parents feel comfortable with what they are doing. Some parents feel happier if they work in a 'backstage' capacity first, making costumes or organising materials where they have an opportunity to observe others at work with the children. Staff should be sensitive to each parent's needs and provide appropriate opportunities for them to become involved.

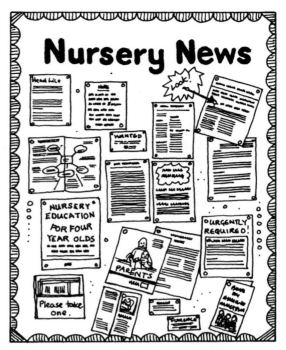

A well-maintained notice board will keep parents informed and will encourage involvement

CASE STUDY

Participating in the curriculum

The playgroup children were working on the theme of buildings. They had looked carefully at the buildings surrounding the centre and had begun making their own model of the local street scene. On a display table was a collection of materials used in buildings, surrounded by a collection of buildings that children had made from Lego and other types of construction material. The staff had put a copy of their planning for the topic on the noticeboard and had asked if parents could contribute in any way. A member of staff knew that one of the parents was a bricklayer and managed to persuade him to come and talk to the children about his work. She asked him to bring along his tools and if possible, demonstrate what he did. The group went out into the corner of the playground and were fascinated by what he showed them. Some children were particularly pleased when they were able to help and pass the tools to him. There were plenty of questions and lots of follow-up play in the play-brick area and at the sand tray. Later that week the group were invited to the building site, where the parent was working, to see a real wall being built.

1 What did the children gain from the experience?
2 What do you think the parent gained from participating in this way?

3 Think of your own centre. How could you involve parents in your current topic or programme?

Taking the curriculum home

Much of children's learning takes place in the home setting where parents' contributions are significant. Most parents will read to their children and encourage them to enjoy stories and rhymes from an early age. Schemes devised by nurseries to involve parents, such as Impact Maths and Science where children and parents are guided through a practical, problem-solving activity, demonstrate this very well. On a less structured basis, everyday tasks and events present learning experiences that parents play a key role in shaping – talking about a television programme, sorting the cutlery in the drawer, watering the plants and so on.

Supporting the centre

Many pre-school centres rely on the support that parents are able to offer them. This may be through their work as unpaid helpers or by collecting materials and equipment to use with the children, or by fund raising. Working closely together in these ways should promote an atmosphere of mutual trust and respect between parents and staff. Social events that get staff and parents together are usually very successful and often raise funds too.

PROGRESS CHECK

1 Why is it important to involve parents in children's learning?
2 How can good relationships with parents be established?
3 What methods can be used to communicate with parents?
4 Parents are often busy people. How can you arrange for all parents to be involved, whatever their responsibilities?

Identifying and meeting training needs

A commitment to developing the skills and expertise of staff through training is an indication of good practice in the pre-school setting. Some centres may find it necessary to alter the focus of their planning and implementation of the curriculum in the light of new or changing requirements. The prospect of change often leads to feelings of anxiety and in this situation the manager of the centre must consider the need for training that will give staff confidence in their abilities to rise to these challenges.

Participation in training should not be seen merely as a way of bringing staff up-to-date. Training that is worthwhile will offer more than that. It will allow practitioners to look critically at their practice and identify strengths and weaknesses in it along with ways of moving forward. At its best, training will fire participants with enthusiasm for the task in hand that will influence the work of colleagues too.

IDENTIFYING NEEDS

It will be helpful to analyse your training needs and this is probably best done by looking at the qualifications and experience of your staff and identifying where there may be a gap. You may find that you can get advice from local bodies – under-eight's officers, the Pre-school Learning Alliance or LEA advisors – about courses that are available.

WHAT TRAINING IS AVAILABLE?

There will be huge variations in what is available according to location. The following are some examples.

- LEAs offer a programmes of in-service training for those working with under-fives. Courses are usually held early evenings, sometimes over a period of weeks. They may be restricted to those working in LEA establishments but some are open to others, often on payment of a higher fee.
- Post-qualification courses are offered by CACHE – the Advanced Diploma in Childcare and Education – and BTEC – the Higher National Certificate in Early Childhood Studies – usually at colleges of Further Education. These require a substantial commitment in terms of cost and time, as they take around two years to complete, but they both contain modules that examine the pre-school curriculum in some depth.
- The Pre-school Learning Alliance offers a range of courses that address aspects of the curriculum aimed at playgroup leaders.
- Associations may publish their own training materials as well as running occasional day schools and lectures for members and for the public. Examples include the British Association for Early Childhood Education (BAECE), the National Children's Bureau, etc.
- In some areas, the under-eights' service provides some training for the centres it registers, though this is becoming rarer.
- The Open University produces some excellent in-service training materials aimed at under-fives' workers.
- Education consultants will offer a range of training options, some tailored to fit your precise needs but often at a price.
- For staff who have no initial childcare qualification, NVQs in childcare and education can be achieved through workplace training and assessment, often with the support of TECs.
- Some Colleges of Further Education and Universities will offer short courses that focus on the curriculum.

OPTIONS FOR TRAINING

It is likely that one of the limitations put on training will be that of the budget so you will have to decide on priorities and criteria. These should be made clear to all staff and allocation of training opportunities must be seen to be fair. One of your criteria is likely to be that the training has an effect on the day-to-day work of the centre. The following are some options.

- Members of staff may be supported to attend training courses on the understanding, when appropriate, that they share ideas and materials with other staff at team meetings. This 'cascading' of information can be very cost-effective but time must be allocated to it.
- Get together with other centres and share expertise. Visits and discussions can provide a new focus and inspire staff to look at things in a different way.
- Join associations that are relevant to your area of work. They often offer training opportunities. Display notices about meetings prominently and refer to them.
- Include professional development as an agenda item at every meeting and organise your own training programme. This works well if someone takes responsibility for planning the programme but all staff can contribute to the delivery by sharing the introduction of topics. For a more structured approach, training materials mentioned above can be used.
- Build up a library of reference books and articles for staff. There are lots of articles in the pre-school press that are relevant and a centre subscription to these publications is a very worthwhile training investment. Circulate articles and discuss at meetings.

GOOD PRACTICE

Opportunities for professional development should be provided for all staff. This may require a number of different approaches, depending on the training priorities identified. The benefits of investing in training will be apparent in the quality of provision through increased knowledge, confidence and motivation on the part of the staff.

PROGRESS CHECK

1 Why should ongoing training be a consideration for all pre-school workers?
2 What kind of training is available?
3 Why is it sometimes difficult for centres to support every training request from staff?

KEY TERMS

You need to know what these words and phrases mean. Go back through the chapter and make sure that you understand:

cascade
cultural diversity
equal opportunities
differentiation
disadvantage
individuality
language diversity
parental involvement
positive images
professional development

racial superiority
role models
self-esteem
special educational needs (SEN)
statement of special educational
    needs
statutory assessment
stereotyping
tokenistic
visual environment

Further reading

Browne, N. and France, P. (eds), *Untying the Apron Strings*, Open University Press, 1986

Dixon, B., *Playing Them False: a study of children's toys, games and puzzles*, Trentham, 1989

Maximé, J., *Black Like Me*, Imani, 1987

Milner, D., *Children and Race: ten years on*, Ward Locke Educational, 1983

Osborn, A.F. and Milbank, J.E., *The Effects of Early Education*, Clarendon Press, 1987

4 PLANNING FOR THE PRE-SCHOOL CURRICULUM

> **This chapter covers:**
> - **The planning and evaluation cycle**
> - **Planning, creating and managing the learning environment**
> - **Observation and assessment**
> - **Record keeping**

The planning and evaluation cycle

Planning is a key factor in the effective implementation of the pre-school curriculum. Careful planning will take into account the learning needs of each individual child within a framework that provides for the delivery of the curriculum to the group. Successful planning should start with the children, with an understanding of their needs and interests and then be developed through themes and activities linked to aspects of the curriculum. Monitoring and evaluation of the implementation process will provide a basis for the next stage of planning.

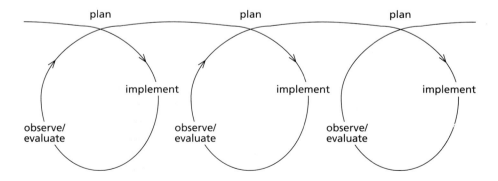

Cycle of planning

THE PLANNING PROCESS

Planning should be meaningful, manageable and useful. Consideration of the following points may contribute to achieving this aim.

Planning as a team

All those who work with the children should participate in the planning process. This will help develop a sense of ownership as everyone will have something to contribute and will ensure a consistent approach. It will also mean that preparation tasks and the gathering of resources can be shared. Students should also be encouraged to contribute to planning as an integral part of their training and they may well bring a different perspective to the procedure. To this end, planning meetings should be scheduled at times when everyone involved is able to attend. Someone needs to take responsibility for organising these meetings and ensuring participation. In some centres this will be the role of a senior member of staff; in others this responsibility may rotate.

CASE STUDY

Planning as a team

The nursery team always got together to plan for their next topic about two months before they intended to introduce it. As the nursery had two job-share nursery nurses, planning and team meetings were arranged for their changeover day, which also happened to be a day when a nursery nurse student was there on placement. At a previous team meeting there had been discussion of a number of possible themes and they had settled on using transport as the focus for the half term's work.

The meeting started with the staff brainstorming ideas and recording these on a flipchart. These suggestions were then mapped to the curriculum areas and looked at carefully. Gaps were identified in some areas and suggestions were made as well as to how the usual activity areas could be used to develop the theme. The group then considered what resources they needed to support the topic. Members of staff volunteered to seek these out, with contacting the library service to order a project collection as a priority. Some trips were suggested and another member of staff said that she would investigate and report back. The nursery nurse student suggested some equipment that she had used at college and said that she would arrange to borrow it and perhaps plan to use it with the children herself. Someone proposed that they reorganise some of the furniture to provide room for another dramatic play area and that was agreed.

New children would be joining the nursery at the beginning of the next half-term and planning for their settling-in period alongside the introduction was also considered. As the meeting drew to a close, the nursery teacher recapped on what had been decided and said that she would provide a copy of the plan for each of the participants and that she would display a version on the nursery noticeboard for parents to see.

The development of the topic was looked at during subsequent team meetings and weekly breakdowns containing more detailed planning were agreed. As the topic got under way some of the original ideas were modified and others included in response to the children's reactions. Parents became involved through lending resources and generally making suggestions. Several offers of help were received including one parent arranging to come and talk about his job as a train driver.

Planning the curriculum as a team

1 Outline the components of planning demonstrated in this case study.
2 Why was this planning so successful?
3 Examine the planning process in your workplace. Could you suggest ways of making it more effective?

Planning and flexibility

Planning should not operate as a straitjacket but should allow for flexibility in responding to children's interests. Sometimes children will respond in a way that you had not anticipated but which is equally valuable. Allow for some spontaneity – the caterpillar truck that comes to dig up the playground provides a stimulus to learning that is too good to miss but you may not have planned for it. Similarly, it would be unwise to deny children the opportunity of playing in the first snow that they have ever seen simply because you had planned something else for that day.

Involving parents

Share your planning with parents. This is particularly important for parents who work alongside you with the children. However, all parents will benefit from knowing what you are working on and may be able to contribute to the learning either with time or resources or by following things through with their children at home. Plans can be displayed in the centre or included in regular newsletters.

Themes and topics
Many pre-school settings plan using themes or topics as a vehicle for integrating different areas of the curriculum. The requirements of the Desirable Outcomes can be successfully incorporated in a thematically planned programme (see page 63). There are several advantages here.

- Children can contribute to the development of the theme through their own interests and experiences.
- Involvement in the theme will promote and sustain children's interest.
- Themes or topics can promote useful links between home and the centre.
- Parents and families can contribute and become involved.
- The theme can provide a unifying focus, linking the different areas of the centre and aspects of the curriculum.

Identifying learning objectives
At each stage of planning, identify content in terms of your expectations of knowledge to be gained, concepts to be developed and skills to be practised, relating these to specific learning objectives.

Plan for individual needs
Consider the needs of all children in your planning and provide for social and emotional as well as intellectual needs. Children who have been assessed as having special educational needs may have Individual Education Plans (IEPs) to be followed and this should be taken into account in planning. Some activities or experiences may require differentiation to ensure that they are appropriate and accessible (see section on SEN, pages 46–49).

Planning for the long, medium and short term
Planning needs to be for the long, medium and short term. Long term planning will require an identification of overall curriculum aims and philosophy and will include the methods that you will use to achieve these aims. For example, if you decided to implement a High Scope approach (see pages 15–17) this would have significant implications for resources, the organisation of the learning environment and training that would need to be addressed in the long term.

Medium term planning will cover a period of weeks, say a term or half-term, developing a theme and associated learning outcomes through a programme of planned and linked experiences.

Short term planning will deal with the day-to-day or week-to-week implementation of those experiences, linking staff and resources to experiences and perhaps identifying particular learning objectives for individual children or groups of children.

Recording planning
Planning needs to be recorded for reference and for accountability. There is no one way of doing this and centres will develop ways of recording their planning that meet their own needs.

ALL ABOUT ME

Language and literacy
- Describing themselves – extend vocabulary for body parts.
- Talking about families and family roles.
- Listening to each other – news and special occasions.
- Stories and rhymes about ourselves include 'head, shoulders, knees and toes' and 'I am sitting, I am sitting'. Also stories about family life and different types of families, e.g. *Alex's Bed*, *Janine and the Baby*, *Alfie* stories.
- Recognising own names and writing them.
- Making 'passports' – write in name, address and age.
- Recognising names of other family members.
- Imaginative play – family play in home corner; baby clinic; and role-play celebration with wedding.
- Also family play in small world.

Physical development
- Moving on particular parts of the body e.g. crawling through barrels; creeping on tip-toes.
- 'Simon says' emphasising body parts.
- Setting individual challenges in out-door play e.g. Can you hop five times? Can you catch a bean-bag? Can you pedal the tricycle?

Personal and social development
- Talking about feelings – describing happy, sad, angry and excited (link to stories).
- Different family styles (link to stories).
- Talk about similarities and differences between ourselves and others.
- Holding a baby – watching a new baby have a bath. (Get Mrs M. to come in.)
- Celebrations – get Rukshana to show us photographs and bring in wedding dress and talk about weddings in Pakistan (link to imaginative play).

Knowledge and understanding of the world

Science
- Exploration of senses – what we can see, taste, touch, hear and smell.
- Looking after living things – ourselves, our pets and plants.
- Parts of the body – joints and making models (linked to technology).

Geography
- Exploring the immediate locality – shops, houses, what else?
- Looking at photographs of local places – can you recognise them?
- Look at different types of buildings and open spaces.

History
- Photo-display of babies – 'look how you've grown!'
- Talking around – 'when I was little, I . . .'.
- Sorting and sequencing photographs of babies, children, adults and old people.
- Looking at old photographs of the locality – what's different?

Technology
- Follow up work on joints by making jointed figures using split pins, hinges and thread.
- Recording own voices (use cassette recorder) – can you recognize the voice?
- Computer programmes – making faces; also, getting dressed.

Mathematics
- Classifying – boys, girls, men and women. Use Logi-people.
- Making sets – brown hair, curly hair, blue eyes, etc.
- Using mathematical language to describe – smaller than, taller than, smallest and tallest.
- Counting up to ten fingers and toes.
- Talking about pairs – of hands, feet, arms and legs. Also socks, shoes and gloves.
- Measuring in handspans and footsteps – making cut-outs of hands and feet and comparing.
- Birthday display – 3s, 4s and 5s in birthday train.
- Recognise own birthday numeral and also house number.

Creative development
- Painting and collage of faces (mix paint for skin tones)
- Full-size paintings of tallest and small-est.
- Songs and rhymes, including action songs.
- Children to choose favourite music at circle time.
- Moving to music – angry music, happy music (linked to PSD on feelings).
- Making music using body sounds – clapping, stamping, tapping and click-ing.
- Making models of own house.

An example of a topic planned around a theme 'All About Me'

Long term planning will be linked to curriculum policy documents, both centre-devised and statutory, and to statements that provide an operational framework for the centre.

Many centres record their medium term planning on topic webs or on grids (see page 65). Here the planning will be organised around developmental and/or curriculum areas and linked to specific activities or experiences. This provides a fairly detailed framework of intentions that might be added to or amended as the topic develops.

Weekly or daily planning can be recorded in a variety of ways using grids, webs, charts or notebooks. In these, specific activities will be indicated alongside resources needed, sometimes with the focus of the activity highlighted.

Members of staff will also plan for work with particular children or groups of children on a week-to-week or day-to-day basis. This short term planning is easily updated if, say, a member of staff is missing or there is an unplanned-for visitor or event. The availability of this planning provides for continuity when regular members of staff are absent and someone else takes over the programme.

> ### Tuesday 22nd. am.
>
> <u>First thing</u> – Speak to Mrs Marshall re. Sean's assessment review
>
> Floating between collage & construction activities. Make sure Lewis & Rowena join in collage
>
> 10.30–11.00 – individual time with Sean. Use cars and bridges, emphasising under & over.
>
> 11.00 – Story time – "The Avocado Baby" – talk about babies & baby food. Finish with "Happy Song" & "Tommy Thumb".
>
> <u>Lunchtime</u>
>
> see Head Teacher re. Sean's SEN assessment.
>
> pm.

An extract from a daily planner

Evaluation

Evaluation is an essential feature of the planning process. It is through continuous observation of children's responses and progress that staff can assess whether their planning and delivery is meeting the needs of the children. This information will enable staff to plan most effectively to meet these changing needs.

TREETOPS NURSERY

Area	Monday	Tuesday	Wednesday	Thursday	Friday
Sand	Dry sand, scoops, buckets and spades, counting scoops	Transparent bottles and boxes, sand-wheel. Focus on pouring	Wet sand – buckets and spades, moulds	Wet sand – play people, farm animals	Wet sand – play people and railway – landscaping
Water	Making boats – corks, paper, card, balsa wood, sticks	Moving boats through water – blowing, agitating water	Beakers, cups, bottles – emphasise full and empty	Teapot and cups – pouring, How many cups?	Washing dolls and dolls clothes – bubbles – keeping clean
Creative	Collage with natural materials – leaves, sticks, cones	Printing with natural materials – leaf shaped paper	Autumn paintings – use brown, yellow, orange	Collage with autumn colours – use matt and shiny	Modelling with boxes – decorating with sticks and seeds
Writing	Dotty paper – hand-eye co-ordination	Threading beads – repeating patterns	Felt tips, pens – writing "messages"	Tracing around shapes	Tracing patterns – left t right – moving across paper
Carpet	Mobilo and play figures	Cars, garage and road lay-out	Cars and roads – duplo houses	Play people and polydrons – emphasise enclosing	Railway track and trains – level crossing and bridges

Many centres use grids for weekly programmes

Effective curriculum planning will put the needs of the individual child at its centre. This will involve consideration of emotional, social and cultural needs alongside curriculum objectives.

PROGRESS CHECK

1 What should be the starting point in planning?
2 Who should be involved in curriculum planning?
3 How can planning be recorded?
4 How does evaluation play a part in planning?

Planning, creating and managing the learning environment

Pre-school centres will find themselves located in a variety of types of accommodation and by no means all will be sited in buildings designed with the needs of children in mind. The challenge to pre-school workers is to plan and create an environment that is interesting and attractive to children and one which enables the curriculum to be delivered in a way that best meets their needs. This section examines three aspects of the learning environment: the physical environment and the organisation of space; the provision of resources; and the role of the adult.

THE PHYSICAL ENVIRONMENT

- The entrance to the centre gives the first impression that parents, children and visitors gain of your work. A welcoming entrance with displays of children's work and interesting and current information about the centre will all contribute to a positive impression. If the entrance is also used as a waiting area and there is space, try to provide some chairs.
- The outdoor area provides for an important aspect of children's learning and should be planned with care. A tarmac or paved space that is large enough for the navigation of wheeled toys should be available and, where possible, a grassy area with space for growing things. Safety will be an important consideration and fences and gates must be secure.
- Cloakrooms, washbasins and lavatories should be easily accessible and child-sized to promote increasing independence.
- Displays can be an important educational tool in the pre-school setting and their use will also add to the attractiveness of the environment. Children's work, well-mounted and displayed with care shows them that you value the children's achievements and enables them to feel positively about these achievements themselves. Displays can be a stimulus to further learning and will also, at a glance, demonstrate to parents and visitors what the children have been working on. Use walls, windows, ceilings, whatever is appropriate in your setting. If you have to

A welcoming entrance creates a positive impression

pack everything away at the end of every session it might be possible to use fold-up screens for display.

GOOD PRACTICE

Displays demonstrate your professional standards to parents, to visitors and, not least, to children. Make sure that the children's work you select to display represents the whole ability range and not just the 'best'. Care should be taken to maintain displays, particularly those in high traffic areas. Displays should be taken down when they are old or faded and when they no longer have a connection with what is going on in the setting and should be replaced with work that is current.

■ Furniture, carpets and curtains will all add to the attractiveness of the environment and make it a pleasant place to work in. In a child-centred environment, these items should be chosen with children in mind, particularly with regard to size and durability.

■ Children need plenty of space in which to play but often a large open space is not conducive to the most purposeful types of play. Providing a number of separate areas for different types of activity through strategic positioning of pieces of

An attractive environment invites children to participate

furniture will enable children to concentrate more readily. This approach allows for flexibility too as the overall make-up of space can be altered easily as required.

CASE STUDY

Organising space for play

A pre-school group was set up in a spare classroom of a local primary school. The room was large and airy and had its own access to an outside play area. The pre-school workers provided a wide range of activities and encouraged children to move freely between them. They noticed that very few of the children settled into the activities for any length of time, with some spending less than a minute at activities. The room seemed very noisy and children were having to be frequently reminded to stop racing around the room.

The pre-school workers decided to borrow some surplus furniture from the school stores and experimented with setting up the room in a different way. Quiet areas such as the book corner and the puzzle table were situated away from the door to the outside play area and the rest of the room was divided into discrete but accessible areas using the furniture as dividers, supplemented by drapes and curtains in some areas. This arrangement gave the impression of separate spaces but allowed the staff to oversee what was going on in each area.

Individual members of staff were allocated to particular activities within the room and were responsible for children working within those areas.

The children stayed longer at the activities and had the opportunity to develop their play there, often supported by an adult. The noise level was affected too as the positioning of the furniture had cut down on the run-through routes and the fabrics absorbed some of the sounds.

1 Look at your own setting. Could you organise the space differently? What effect would this have?

Space should be organised so that all children can participate fully

- The space should be organised so that all children can participate fully. You may need to make adjustments for, say, a child who is blind or one who uses a wheel-chair.
- Paint, clay, sand and water need to be near sinks where possible and on safe and durable floor covering.
- Keeping doors and windows accessible should be a consideration, as should the need for children to circulate freely within the area.
- In centres where meals are served, thought should be given to provision of a dining area. Children staying for day long sessions may also require an appropriate space for rest and sleep.

GOOD PRACTICE

The physical environment must be a safe place for children and adults. Health and Safety regulations must be adhered to with staff taking responsibility, checking the premises for hazards regularly and ensuring prompt action is taken where necessary.

PROVIDING AND ORGANISING RESOURCES

- Most pre-school centres would include provision for activities in the following educational areas:
  - a creative or craft area, to include a range of activities
  - a construction area for both large and small equipment
  - provision for role play, including other kinds of socio-dramatic play as well as home-corner play
  - an area for malleable materials such as dough, clay, Plasticine, etc
  - miniature world play such as play people, farms, cars, dolls' houses, etc.
  - outdoor play, to include imaginative play as well as climbing, running, pedalling, etc.
  - puzzles and games
  - natural materials such as sand, water, clay, earth and wood
  - a writing area where children experiment with different writing media and use writing meaningfully
  - a book area
  - an area for technology including, in some centres, provision for information technology
  - an area for larger group interaction, often the home carpet or corner.

  It is through these areas of activity that all aspects the curriculum can be presented to children in a way that takes into account their individual capabilities and preferences.
- The resources provided for use in the above areas should support the full range of learning needs. Variety in provision will maintain interest in the area. However this should be balanced by children's need to become familiar and confident in using certain types of resources. For example if Lego is offered only occasionally in the interests of variety then children will not have sufficient opportunity to explore all its possibilities.
- Staff should decide on spending priorities when it comes to resource allowances as some areas may require more substantial and expensive attention than others.
- Criteria need to be set when selecting resources. Safety will obviously be a primary concern as will quality and durability. Equipment that can be used in a variety of ways will provide for versatility and is good value for money when budgets are limited. Consideration should be given to the promotion of equal opportunities through the selection of resources (see pages 38–45).
- Organisation of resources is an important consideration. A High Scope delivery of the curriculum (see pages 15–17) will require resources to be organised in a way that allows children to select the items they need and then return them to their place after use. Whatever the method of curriculum delivery, children will become more independent if they are able to locate the equipment they need and if they are involved in putting it away afterwards. To this end, it will be helpful if resources are stored where they are accessible to children and labelled appropriately.
- Resources need to be regularly maintained, cleaned and checked for damage. Anything that is incomplete, unhygienic or beyond repair should be discarded.

THE ROLE OF THE ADULT

The role of the adult in managing the learning environment could be summarised as follows.

- To plan and prepare the environment so that it meets the individual learning needs of each child in the group.
- To be aware of the learning opportunities that each activity provides.
- To welcome and encourage children to the session and into specific activities.
- To interact with children in ways that focus on the learning potential of the materials and activity.
- To provide for balance in the range of activities experienced by individual children. This will involve monitoring children's choices and encouraging them into activities that are generally avoided.
- To observe and evaluate the response to activities and to use this in future planning.
- To supervise the area and maintain safety during the session.
- To ensure that all children can join in and that none are intimidated or bullied.
- To monitor noise levels so that the atmosphere is conducive to purposeful play.
- To care for the learning environment so that it continues to offer a welcoming and stimulating experience.

GOOD PRACTICE

Children gain a great deal from the involvement of adults in their play. Childcare workers should watch children closely and take every opportunity to involve themselves as appropriate.

PROGRESS CHECK

1 What considerations should be borne in mind when planning the learning environment?
2 How can the organisation of the learning environment promote children's independence?
3 How does the organisation of the learning environment influence the curriculum and the curriculum influence the learning environment?
4 Outline the role of the adult in managing the learning environment.

Observation and assessment

Observation should be seen as an integral part of the role of pre-school workers, as a professional skill that enables them to map the progress of children and to plan for the next stage. Adults in pre-school settings are observing and responding to their observations in an intuitive way all the time – perhaps observing that a child has fallen over and offering comfort or observing that the paper tray is empty and refilling it. However, observation that has a clear focus and purpose will be more rewarding as it will identify the particular needs of children as well as strengths and weaknesses in your provision.

Observations should be objective. If you approach a child or a situation with a pre-conceived idea of what you expect to find, then this will influence what you see and undermine the validity of your observation.

What do you observe?
- Observe individual children during their play. You may want to focus on general development or an area of concern. All children will benefit from the attention of observation, not just those about whom you have a concern.
- Observe children in groups and look at interaction and cooperation.
- Consider a piece of equipment and see how children respond to it.
- Map children's pathways around the room. Are some areas avoided?

When can you observe?
Centres will vary as to how they incorporate observation into their routine but it should be a regular feature. In some cases one member of staff will take responsibility for observing while others support the session and interact with the children, although in many centres observation will take place alongside and with other duties.

RECORDING OBSERVATIONS

Devise methods of recording observations that are unobtrusive and match your purpose. For example, if you are observing the movement of children around the classroom, then a sketch of the layout would be useful. Checklists that are easy to fill in can be devised for many purposes. If you are interested in language interaction in the home corner, then you may wish to use a small tape recorder. At other times, a small notebook and pencil will be the most appropriate equipment.

SHARING OBSERVATIONS

Observations should be discussed with colleagues and perhaps put into a wider context before decisions are taken on any action that might be necessary. Including students in these discussions is often worthwhile as they will be making regular observations as part of their training and it will help them to understand the importance of this skill in their practice. Observations can form part of discussions with parents when they can be compared with parents' own observations of their child. They may also be shared with other professionals as part of an ongoing assessment process.

CASE STUDY

Using observation
Alex had been attending nursery for about six months. At this nursery, staff make focused observations of individual children on a regular basis and discuss their findings at team meetings. The general feeling was that

Alex had settled well and enjoyed most activities. The nursery nurse observed Alex for the whole of a morning session, focusing on his social interactions with other children and on the areas of activity he chose to play in. She found that although he appeared to be part of a group, for much of the time he was watching others play and was not able to take a real part in the activity. He chose a range of activities but during that session avoided painting and craft. This observation was discussed at the team meeting with other staff. They had seen him obviously engrossed in painting and craft on other occasions and did not feel his missing those activities this time was significant. However, they felt that he did need a chance to break into group play and suggested that a member of staff play alongside Alex in a group and encourage him to be more assertive. At the next meeting, they would review the situation and decide whether there was still cause for concern.

1 Why was focused observation useful in this situation?
2 What pre-conceived ideas might the staff have had about Alex?
3 In your own work setting, what use do you make of observation?

EVALUATING OBSERVATION

On an individual basis, evaluation of observations will reveal the child's learning potential and can help to assess the progress achieved. More widely, evaluating provision through observation will demonstrate how effectively plans are being implemented and the intended learning objectives being achieved. Staff can then plan for subsequent sessions making any necessary adjustments in organisation, resources, interaction and expectations on the basis of these evaluations.

PROGRESS CHECK

1 Why is observation such an important professional skill?
2 Identify some ways in which you can record observations.
3 Why should observations have a focus?

Record keeping

All centres will need to keep records about individual children and their progress. Most will use a range of different types of records, each type with a distinct purpose. Record-keeping can take up a significant amount of time and effort and it is up to pre-school workers to ensure that the records they compile are appropriate and that they are productive.

Why do we keep records?
■ To build up a picture of each individual child.
■ To monitor individual progress in all areas of development and, in the light of this, to plan for the child's future progress.
■ To help evaluate provision and contribute to planning. Record-keeping will also

highlight the difference between what we expect children to learn and what they actually do learn.

- To communicate with staff and other professionals.
- To share children's achievements and progress with parents.
- To provide for continuity from one centre to the next.
- To demonstrate accountability. Records can be used to explain and justify the work that you do.

To be useful, records need to be both accurate and current, with entries dated and signed by the person who is making them. This might be more manageable if each member of staff has overall responsibility for the records of a small group of children.

TYPES OF RECORDS

- A profile of the child will usually be compiled with parents on admission to a centre. This often entails working through a list outlining aspects of development and will include the child's preferences and any other related information. This provides an opportunity for parents to become involved in the record-keeping process from the very beginning. These profiles will serve as a starting point and will be added to by staff and parents as they gain more knowledge about the child (see page 75). Some local authorities require their centres to complete a standard profile as part of base-line assessment programmes (see pages 76–77).
- Written observations are an important element in record-keeping. They provide detailed information about a child in the everyday context of their play. Such observations enable staff to see the child as a whole rather than as a list of skills or behaviour achieved, or not. Regular observation over a period of time will provide a very detailed picture of the child.
- Checklists can be used for a variety of purposes. They are used to record developmental achievements, for example 'she can build a tower with three bricks' or to map children's involvement in activities. Some checklists break down a certain area such as reading, for example, into individual elements and progress can be charted stage by stage (see pages 75 and 78). Checklists are quick and easy to fill in and children and parents will enjoy seeing progress recorded. However, checklists on their own will not give a complete picture of the child.
- Portfolios or records of achievement in the form of selected examples of children's work (or photographs of work), dated and collected over a period of time will provide evidence of progression and become a focus of pride for parents and for children. Comments by staff, parents or the child can also be added, placing the work in its context. Portfolios can then be passed on to the next centre that the child attends. One problem with portfolios is that they tend to grow very quickly and present difficulties for storage.

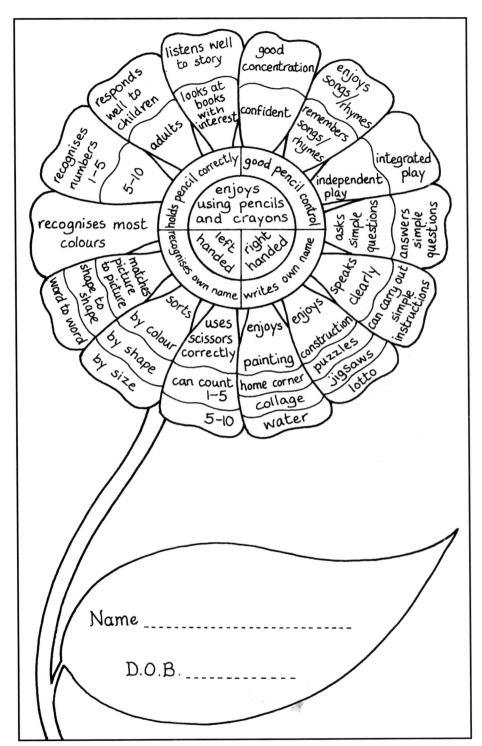

Staff and parents can fill in sections as the child's skills develop

Entry & Baseline assessment

		Nursery 1	Nursery 2	Baseline	KS1 TA
Age		:	:	:	:
Date of Assessment		:	:	:	:
SOCIAL DEVELOPMENT					
A yet to develop/be observed	*Interaction*				
B observes others rather than participating					
C usually chooses to work/play alone					
D engages in parallel activity with others					
E engages in co-operative activity with others; shares and takes turns					
A yet to develop/be observed	*Concentration*				
B very short attention span					
C attention span limited with directed tasks					
D generally concentrates well with directed and non-directed tasks					
E consistently concentrates until activity concluded					
A yet to develop/be observed	*Motivation*				
B always needs an adult to start on a task					
C selects own tasks; will engage on a favourite task or activity without an adult					
D actively engages in a variety of tasks without adult direction					
E asks many questions; interested in most tasks					
PHYSICAL DEVELOPMENT					
A yet to develop/be observed	*Fine Motor*				
B uses palm grasp					
C uses pincer grasp; handles small objects					
D uses small tools and equipment purposefully eg scissors					
E uses small tools and equipment with control					
A yet to develop/be observed	*Gross Motor*				
B negotiates way round spaces in room					
C uses a range of equipment eg large construction					
D uses a range of equipment with control					
E shows co-ordination in running, catching, balance, throwing, kicking, hopping					
LITERACY					
A yet to develop/be observed	*En 1 Speaking*				
B uses sounds and/or gestures to communicate meaning					
C speaks to peers and adults					
D initiates conversation with peers and adults					
E conveys simple meaning audibly and can extend accounts with detail (L1)					
A yet to develop/be observed	*En 1 Listening*				
B responds to actions/stories/songs/rhymes					
C listens attentively to short stories					
D follows a two-step instruction					
E listens to others and usually responds appropriately; takes simple messages (L1)					

This entry and baseline assessment has been devised by Nottinghamshire LEA. It can be used at entry to nursery at 3 years (Nursery 1) or 4 years (Nursery 2) as

Entry & Baseline assessment

	Nursery 1	Nursery 2	Baseline	KS1 TA
Age	:	:	:	:
Date of Assessment	:	:	:	:

LITERACY *continued*

	En 2 Reading				
A yet to develop/be observed					
B shows some interest in books					
C recognises that books have a purpose					
D recognises that print conveys meaning					
E recognises individual words or letters in familiar context (L1)					
A yet to develop/be observed *En 3 Writing*					
B uses pictures and/or marks to communicate					
C uses symbols and/or individual letters to communicate meaning					
D writes single words without a model					
E communicates meaning through simple written words and phrases (L1)					

MATHEMATICS

A yet to develop/be observed *Ma 1 Using & Applying*				
B matches simple objects				
C sorts using own attribute/s				
D uses equipment and maths knowledge to solve a task, with help				
E decides how to tackle a task and talks about what she/he has found using mathematics as an integral part of activities (L1)				
A yet to develop/be observed *Ma 2 Number*				
B can say numbers to at least 5				
C uses counting equipment; counts sets 1:1 to at least 5				
D recognises numbers 1-10; counts and orders to 10; adds to 5 using apparatus				
E counts, orders, adds and subtracts numbers in problems involving up to 10 objects (L1)				
A yet to develop/be observed *Ma 2 Algebra*				
B copies patterns of two colours or objects				
C continues a pattern using 2 colours or objects				
D continues a pattern using 3 or 4 colours or objects				
E recognises and devises repeating patterns, counting the numbers in each repeat (L1)				
A yet to develop/be observed *Ma 3 Shape & Space*				
B sorts square, rectangle, triangle, circle by shape				
C recognises and names square, rectangle, triangle, circle				
D understands words commonly used to describe simple properties of space and shape				
E uses everyday language to describe 2D and 3D properties and positions (L1)				

well as at entry to school at 5 years (Baseline) and at 7 years (at the end of Key Stage 1)

As reading skills develop parents and staff can complete the jigsaw

SHARING RECORDS

- Records should be shared with other members of the team as they have implications for everyone who works with the children.
- Other professionals, such as the speech therapist or ESL (English as a Second Language) assistant who work with the child will need access to records and the opportunity to contribute to them.
- A great deal is to be gained from sharing records with parents. From the beginning, parents make initial contributions to children's records when they pass on information at admission. They have much to add from their own observations of their children outside the centre, putting the child into the wider context.

Information about children's achievements or concerns is often exchanged informally at the beginning or end of sessions and this can work very well. However, there is a place for a more structured exchange of information where records can be updated by parents and by staff and progress discussed. The starting point for these discussions will be the information contained in the different records, giving parents an opportunity to add their views and supplement with additional information. Plans for continuing progress can also be discussed with parents, emphasising the partnership between home and centre and recognising the parents' key role in their children's learning.

Written reports to parents on children's progress are less common for this age group. Most pre-school staff would prefer to meet with parents and exchange information about the child's progress. However, some centres provide written comments to parents and ask parents to respond to these.

CASE STUDY

Sharing record keeping with parents

The family centre had introduced a system of open profiles for all the children in the centre. A large format folder was provided for each child, personalised with a photograph on the cover. At their child's admission parents were told about the profiles, given a booklet outlining the aims of the scheme, which were that parents, staff and children would all contribute to the profiles, and given guidance about how to go about filling them in.

The profiles were stored in a large open bookcase and were always available to parents. Key workers were responsible for updating the profiles of their children on a regular basis and for acting on information gleaned from them. Staff also organised a regular monthly profile session where parents were encouraged to stay and spend time working on the profiles and talking things through with staff. Parents also spent time with children, helping select work to add to the profiles and writing the child's comments alongside. The team evaluated the project after six months. They agreed that the gains had been significant for all parties involved. Staff had access to much more information about the children and had greater respect for parents. Parents gained a clearer understanding of the way that the centre operated and were made aware of their contribution to their children's learning. Children had the opportunity to see their parents working closely together with centre workers and had the benefit of extra adult attention.

1 What were the benefits of this initiative?
2 Can you think of any disadvantages?
3 How does your centre involve parents in contributing to and sharing records?

Parents can help children select more to include in their personal profiles

PROGRESS CHECK

1 Why is keeping records important for childcare workers?
2 What kinds of records are useful?
3 Who should contribute to records about children's progress?

KEY TERMS

You need to know what these words and phrases mean. Go back through the chapter and make sure that you understand:

accountability
base-line assessment
checklists
differentiation
High Scope
integrating areas of the curriculum
learning objectives
learning potential

malleable materials
monitoring and evaluation
portfolios
pre-conceived idea
socio-dramatic play
themes and topics
topic webs

PART TWO
The Pre-school Curriculum

5 PERSONAL AND SOCIAL DEVELOPMENT

This chapter covers:
- How Personal and Social Development underpins the pre-school curriculum
- Developing self esteem
- Developing independence
- Developing interpersonal skills
- Developing an awareness of morality
- Further reading

Personal and Social Development is concerned with the skills and attitudes that enable a child to develop a strong sense of self worth and become a successful member of society. In the pre-school curriculum the focus is on children learning how to function in a social group beyond the family in the context of personal and social values. DfEE with SCAA (1996) outline the basis of this:

> *Children are confident, show appropriate self respect and are able to establish effective relationships with other children and with adults. They work as part of a group and independently, are able to concentrate and persevere in their learning and to seek help when needed. They are eager to explore new learning, and show the ability to initiate new ideas and to solve simple practical problems. They demonstrate independence in selecting an activity or resources and in dressing and personal hygiene.*
>
> *Children are sensitive to the needs and feelings of others and show respect for people of other cultures and beliefs. They take turns and share fairly. They express their feelings and behave in appropriate ways, developing an understanding of what is right and wrong and why. They treat living things properly and their environment with care and concern. They respond to relevant cultural and religious events and show a range of feelings, such as wonder, joy or sorrow, in response to their experiences of the world.*
>
> (Desirable Outcomes for Children's Learning, *DfEE with SCAA, 1996*)

How Personal and Social Development underpins the pre-school curriculum

Personal and Social Development permeates the whole pre-school curriculum. It is not a discrete subject area in itself but concerned with the skills and attitudes that enable children to develop a strong sense of their own worth and become successful members of society. As these are important aspects of a children's learning and development, and have an impact on their ability to learn, it is important that issues of personal and social development are considered by the staff team and are not left to individuals and to chance.

Personal and social skills and attitudes are learned in daily interaction with other people. They are acquired from the ethos of an establishment and in the attitudes of staff. Mead (1934) used the term 'significant others' to describe the people who influence a child's attitudes and social behaviour. Significant others include:

- parents
- other family members
- friends and peers
- childcare workers and teachers.

Concentric circles of socialization (Bronfenbremer, 1975)

The attitudes of a childcare worker are very important in a child's personal and social development. Young children are very dependent upon adults and this, coupled with their immature ability to reason, means that these early messages become internalised by children and form the basis of their attitudes. These attitudes are communicated in the daily interactions with others. This is sometimes described as a 'looking glass self': we are a reflection of the people with whom we interact. Through these daily interactions children build up a picture of themselves and their place in the wider society. There is evidence to suggest that children who develop a positive sense of their own worth and their place in society are successful within the education system and beyond. The two following points are, therefore, important for childcare workers to take into account.

1 Childcare workers should know how a positive sense of self, others and society can be developed. These issues are dealt with in this chapter.

2 Childcare workers should consider their own attitudes and skills that may affect the children in their care. This requires an awareness that their own attitudes may be stereotypical and, therefore, limiting to the children in their care. For example, childcare workers may have the views that children from a socially deprived area will be low achievers or that boys do not like to play with dolls. Both these beliefs will be reflected in their attitudes and communicated to the children. Children's choices, both within the pre-school setting and later, beyond schooling, are then limited by assumptions made about them. Each child needs to be recognised as an individual who brings a complex range of experiences to the learning environment.

CASE STUDY

Communicating expectations

Tom and Hannah arrived in the nursery wearing new shoes. They were both keen to show the staff their shoes.

Tom: 'Do you like my shoes?'

Adult: 'Yes they're lovely, they look like new shoes, all clean and shiny.'

Tom: 'Yes, they are new and I'm going to wear them to play outside.'

Adult: 'Well I bet they won't stay clean and shiny for long when you are outside'.

Hannah: 'Do you like my shoes?'

Adult: 'Yes, they're lovely. Tom has got some new shoes as well. They're like yours, all clean and shiny.'

Hannah: 'I can wear them outside to play.'

Adult: 'Yes, you'll have to be careful outside if you want to keep them clean and shiny.'

These are similar conversations, superficially about children's new shoes. However, messages about our expectations of girls and boys are evident in the words and phrases used. Tom is not expected to take responsibility for keeping his shoes clean and shiny. It is seen as inevitable that they will get dirty. This is evident when the adult says 'I bet they won't stay clean and shiny for long when you are outside.' In contrast, Hannah is expected to take some responsibility for keeping her shoes clean and shiny. The adult's response to her is, 'You'll have to be careful outside if you want to keep them clean and shiny.'

1 What do these responses indicate about the expectations of girls and boys?
2 What information may be communicated to each child through this interaction with the adult?
3 What impact may this have on their play outside?
4 What stereotypical views, of both girls and boys behaviour, does this reinforce?
5 How could the adult have interacted with both these children in a more positive, and less limiting, way?

PROGRESS CHECK

1 What is personal and social development?
2 Explain why personal and social development permeates the whole pre-school curriculum.
3 How do children develop personal and social skills and attitudes?
4 What is a 'significant other'?
5 Who are the significant others in children's lives?
6 What is 'the looking glass self'?
7 How can childcare workers ensure that they are able to meet the needs of young children in this important area of development?

Developing self esteem

Self esteem is an individual's assessment of their worth. It develops from birth during interaction with other people. It is important as it affects our outlook on life and can determine what we try and, therefore, what we achieve. Self esteem is established at a young age and research evidence shows that it remains stable throughout life, so it is vital that positive self esteem is established while children are young.

It is important to recognise that the only way children are able to perceive themselves is through the way that others respond to them. For example a child who receives praise for trying a new task is more likely to continue to persist at a task than a child who is told that they have got it wrong.

WHAT IS SELF ESTEEM?

Self concept
During their early years children develop a complex series of concepts about themselves. They begin to define themselves in terms of how others see them. Some of these concepts are defined categories recognised within society: child, sister, wheelchair user, girl, Sikh. Others are more personal: likeable, clever, well behaved, a good reader. These reflected roles come together to form our self concept. This self concept is different for each person as their interactions are all slightly different.

Ideal self

Alongside an individual's self concept, each person also develops a concept of an ideal self. This is a series of expectations, that are communicated to individuals through social interactions that contain messages about what is acceptable in both societal and individual terms.

Self esteem

The self concept – what we understand ourselves to be – is measured against the ideal self – what we think we should be. The individual's assessment of the difference between these two forms their self esteem. When these two are similar an individual is said to have a high self esteem – to feel good about themselves. When there is a large gap between the two an individual is said to have a low self esteem – not to feel good about themselves.

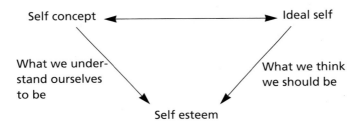

An individual's assessment of the difference between self concept and ideal self

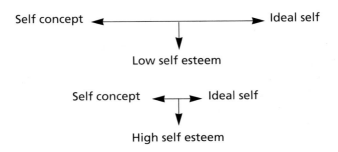

How self esteem is acquired

This is, of course, a simplified version of how self esteem is acquired. Social interaction is extremely complex and because of personality each person's experiences are different. A person may have a global self esteem that is high but in some aspects of their life, perhaps where they lack confidence or are dependent upon a particular person and/or situation, their self esteem in this particular area may be low, although in general they feel good about themselves.

BEHAVIOURAL IMPLICATIONS OF SELF ESTEEM

Coopersmith (Maccoby 1980) cites research evidence of how high and low self esteem is reflected in children's behaviour. The results show that there is a direct contrast between the two groups. In a comparative analysis of children with high and low self esteem, children with high self esteem had the following profile:

- they would approach tasks with the expectation that they would be well received and successful
- they had confidence in their perceptions and judgements and believed that they could succeed
- they accepted their own opinions as valid and placed trust in their own reactions and conclusions
- they were willing to consider novel ideas
- they would express their opinions
- they demonstrated good social independence and creativity
- they were more likely to be participators rather than listeners in a group situation
- they reported less difficulty in forming friendships
- overall they lacked self consciousness and pre-occupation with personal problems.

In contrast children with low self esteem showed greater difficulty in acquiring all these attitudes and skills.

It can be seen from the list that high self esteem has a profound impact on all aspects of the children's lives. This influence is likely to extend beyond formal education. It is evident that developing a positive self esteem is an important part of personal and social development.

GOOD PRACTICE IN DEVELOPING SELF ESTEEM

Because young children can only perceive themselves through the way that others respond to them it is important that adults who work with children respond in a positive way. The following are some of the ways in which this can be achieved in a childcare setting.

Interaction with children
- Demonstrate love and affection to all children.
- Demonstrate respect for children.
- Provide children with a stimulating, developmentally appropriate activities
- Give children manageable tasks but also be aware when a child is ready for new challenges.
- Encourage children to be self dependent and responsible.
- Encourage children to do as much as possible for themselves.
- Encourage children to persevere and complete tasks and activities.

Managing behaviour
- Use 'do' rather 'don't' in managing children's behaviour. This emphasises what you want the child to do rather than what is not acceptable.
- Explain why rules exist and why children must adhere to them.

- Give appropriate praise, for effort as much as for achievement.
- Be on the child's side. Assume that a child means to do right not wrong.

Creating a positive ethos and environment
- Encourage a child to use language to express their feelings as well as all other needs.
- Be interested in what children say. Actively listen and offer your own experiences and opinions.

Listening carefully demonstrates that you are interested in what children say

- Be a good role model. Demonstrate that you value and respect other people.
- Provide positive role models for all children with regard to gender, ethnicity, disability.
- Encourage children to value who they are with regard, for example, to their cultural background or their gender.
- Provide children with the opportunity for role play where they can experiment with different roles.
- Provide children with their own things, labelled with their name.

Most importantly this approach to children must be consistent. The consistency must be evident from all staff at all times. It cannot depend upon which staff are working and how they are feeling, therefore, all staff members need to be aware of their interactions with children, and staff development time needs to be given to understanding and refining skills in this important area of development.

Demonstrating respect for children

Musrat, a nursery nurse, was engaged in a conversation with a child. Another member of staff came into the room and called across to Musrat asking her to help find the new paints. Musrat placed her hand on the child's arm, told her colleague that it would be a little while until she could help her and returned to the conversation with the child.

Simple, everyday incidents like this can have an impact on how children perceive themselves. In this example Musrat demonstrated her respect for the child by prioritising the conversation with the child over the demands of another member of staff. From this incident the child is likely to feel valued by a significant other. This is a contributory factor in developing a high self-esteem.

1 How did Musrat demonstrate respect for the child?
2 Why do you think it was important for Musrat to maintain physical contact with the child while she quickly answered her colleague?
3 What messages may the child have picked up had Musrat broken off their conversation mid-way through and gone to look for the paint?
4 What other, everyday incidents can you identify that may have an impact on how children perceive themselves?

PROGRESS CHECK

1 What is self esteem?
2 Why is a positive self esteem important?
3 Why are other people important in the development of an individual's self esteem?
4 What is self concept?
5 What is an ideal self?
6 How do these affect self esteem?
7 Describe good practice in developing a child's self esteem.

Developing independence

Babies are completely dependent upon adults for their every need, but throughout childhood children gradually become less dependent upon adults. This begins in early childhood by children becoming physically less dependent upon adults. As they grow and learn they begin to gain experiences and form relationships beyond their immediate family, becoming more emotionally and socially independent. Gaining this independence is an important aspect of a child's development. Tina Bruce (1991) argues that this sense of control over their own lives impinges upon children's self esteem. In turn this affects an individual's self confidence, autonomy, intrinsic motivation, desire to 'have a go' and take risks, ability to solve problems and, therefore, to take decisions and to choose.

Initially, children will develop skills that enable them to become less physically dependent upon adults. This includes skills such as:

- eating independently
- toileting
- washing and dressing themselves.

If the development of these skills is handled sensitively this independence will enable children to feel more confident about themselves and begin the process of becoming self reliant. Children who have confidence in their ability to manage their physical needs can than build on these skills. This will enable them to make full use of the experiences on offer to them. In a childcare setting the next stage of independence may include development of the following skills:

- selecting an activity
- selecting resources
- asking for help when needed
- initiating ideas
- solving simple problems.

GOOD PRACTICE IN DEVELOPING INDEPENDENCE SKILLS

There are a number of important points for the childcare worker to consider in developing children's independence skills.

Time
Children need the time to practice and refine their developing skills and this must be recognised in the planning and organisation of activities and experiences. This not only includes time to complete physical tasks but time to explore new experiences and relationships. It may involve the child observing other children. This is a necessary part of development – children need time to stand and stare so that they can make sense of all the new experiences in their life.

Praise
Young children's lives are awash with new experiences and skills that they need to acquire. Appropriate praise, coupled with appropriate intervention will encourage a child to persevere. Praise should be given as much for trying as for succeeding.

Intervention that enables a child to succeed
Sometimes children may need to be shown how to do something that enables them to become more independent, for example, to tie shoe laces. They are not likely to discover how do this without any input from someone else! Success needs to be built into showing children how to do things, otherwise they are likely to become frustrated. This is usually achieved through a step-by-step approach. The task needs to by broken down into small steps and each step practised separately.

A clear routine
Routine enables a child to be able to predict what is likely to happen. This consistency fosters feelings of security. A secure environment is necessary for children to

explore all the unknowns that they will undoubtedly come across. This exploration is necessary for a child to become a confident, independent member of the group.

CASE STUDY

Adult intervention that enables a child to succeed

A new role play area was set up as a café. The children had looked at books, discussed what was needed, collected the equipment and helped to set the area up. When the children began to play in the area a playworker noticed that Firzana was hovering at the edges of the play. She did not get involved in the play but it was clear that she would like to. The playworker asked Firzana if she would like to come to the café with her. They went into the café and ordered some food. As they were waiting Firzana said that she wanted to be a waitress. The playworker, keeping in role, asked if there were any jobs at the café for two new waitresses. She then suggested that as new waitresses they needed some training and the other children showed them what to do. The playworker and Firzana then spent some time as waitresses in the café.

The following day the playworker observed Firzana playing in the café as a waitress. She was observed discussing how she had just started to work at the café and how she had been trained for the job.

Adults can intervene in children's play to enable a child to be successful

The playworker's intervention enabled Firzana to successfully engage in imaginative play. Through this intervention Firzana became more independent in her learning and was, therefore, able to make the most of the opportunities on offer to her. This was evident the following day when she was able to select this activity and initiate her own play themes.

1 How did the playworker intervene without making the child feel exposed?
2 Why is the ability to select and initiate play experiences an important part of a child's development?
3 In what ways did this child demonstrate greater independence skills?

PROGRESS CHECK

1 Why is it important that children become independent from their carers?
2 What aspects of independence are developing at pre-school age?
3 Why is it important that this development is handled in a sensitive way?
4 What are the important considerations in developing a child's independence skills?

Developing interpersonal skills

Interpersonal skills are the skills that enable us to get along with other people. These skills are learned. In the main they are learned through interaction with other people. Piaget describes young children as being egocentric. That means that they find it difficult to see the world from another's point of view. It is important to realise this is not the same as being selfish, being selfish means that you can see other points of view and yet choose your own. Good interpersonal skills require a person to have social empathy – to be able to tune into other people's feelings and viewpoints and act accordingly. Children need to learn to do this.

At pre-school age the skills that children are developing include:

- forming friendships
- maintaining friendships
- sharing
- taking turns
- responding appropriately to others
- becoming sensitive to other people's feelings
- expressing a range of feelings appropriately
- beginning to develop appropriate patterns of behaviour.

GOOD PRACTICE IN DEVELOPING INTERPERSONAL SKILLS

There are a number of important considerations for the childcare worker in developing children's interpersonal skills.

Pre-school-aged children need to learn to develop and maintain friendships

Role models

Children learn successful interpersonal skills from the people that they interact with. Children model their behaviour on what they experience. It is, therefore, necessary for childcare workers to provide good role models for all the children in their care. This must be evident in both adult with adult interactions and adult with child interactions.

A child needs to see adults, in their interactions, actions and attitudes, demonstrating:

- respect for others – both adults and children
- sensitivity towards others' feelings
- respect for all cultures, beliefs and ways of life.

This behaviour must be consistent and constant and can be achieved by careful planning to ensure consistency, for example by:

- ensuring that displays reflect cultural diversity
- not assuming all children live in a nuclear family
- ensuring that all children's names are pronounced correctly and finding out how parents want to be addressed
- agreeing how to address another, either by name, title or otherwise
- recognising that children's conversation is as important as adults' and should not be interrupted
- maintaining a policy of asking for and, where appropriate, acting upon children's views and opinions.

Encouragement

Children also need the opportunity to develop skills of sharing and turn taking. Opportunities for this arise throughout the session, for example sharing paint pots, construction equipment and bikes. Children need to be reminded and encouraged to share and take turns. This is not easy for children who, at this age, tend to be egocentric. In some instances there may need to be systems set up to ensure that all children are able to have a turn where, for example, the number of bikes within an establishment is limited. Staff must ensure that all the children, who want to, are able to have a turn, and not only the same few children who always seem to get to them first!

Rewards

Praise, for behaviour that is appropriate and that you want the children to repeat, is another way in which children are able to understand what is acceptable and what is not. This praise should be directed at an individual when they do exhibit appropriate behaviour. Also praise can be directed away from a child. If a child is exhibiting inappropriate behaviour, praise can be offered to another child or group of children who are behaving appropriately. This has the benefits of demonstrating to the child what behaviour you do want to see and also shows the child that appropriate behaviour gets attention, rather than inappropriate behaviour.

There will be situations where a child needs to be encouraged to displace inappropriate behaviour with appropriate behaviour through good role models and intervention with a system of rewards and sanctions.

CASE STUDY

Being a positive role model

A nursery nurse and a group of children were reading a book together. They were half way through when another child, in her eagerness to get a piece of construction equipment, fell onto the bricks and began to cry. The nursery nurse had to stop reading the story and go to the distressed child. She quickly explained to the group that she must comfort the child but she would come back. Within a few minutes the nursery nurse was back with the group, with the child on her knee. She apologised to the group for leaving them and asked them why they thought she had to leave the story. The group talked about being hurt and needing to be comforted and how that had to be done immediately rather than at the end of a story. The nursery nurse then read the story to the group.

In this situation the adult provided a positive role model for the children. As well as demonstrating concern for the distressed child she showed respect for the original group, first by apologising and then by finishing the original activity. She also encouraged the children to empathise with the distressed child and show sensitivity towards another's feelings. They were able to recognise that their needs came second for a short period of time. This skill is a difficult one for young children who tend to be egocentric and who tend to live in the 'here and now' and cannot defer gratification.

1 What messages may the children have picked up from the nursery nurse's actions?

2 Why is it important that they understand the nursery nurse's actions?

3 In what ways might this learning affect the children's behaviour towards one another?

4 Why is sensitivity towards others difficult for young children?

PROGRESS CHECK

1 What are interpersonal skills?

2 Why are interpersonal skills important?

3 How are interpersonal skills learned?

4 Young children tend to be egocentric. Why is this an important consideration in the development of children's interpersonal skills?

5 Why are good role models important?

6 How can childcare workers provide good role models?

7 Describe how a childcare worker can provide encouragement for a child to share and take turns.

8 How can praise help a child develop acceptable patterns of behaviour?

9 Give some examples of praise used to develop acceptable patterns of behaviour in children.

Developing an awareness of morality

Morality is concerned with an understanding of right and wrong. Also, very importantly, why things are considered to be right or wrong. Morality is closely linked with the interpersonal skill of being sensitive towards others. A strong sense of social empathy will enable a child to see the impact of their actions and attitudes upon other people. It is important to be sensitive to the fact that there will be children who come from different traditions, different cultures and religious backgrounds and that they may bring with them different moral traditions and mores. This must be considered when discussing, planning and assessing the curriculum.

MORAL DEVELOPMENT

Young children think in different ways to older children and adults (see pages 19–24). They cannot, therefore, be expected to consider their actions and attitudes, and their impact upon others, in the same way as older children and adults. This is evident in the stages of moral development.

Kohlberg's six stages of moral development

Kohlberg (1969, 1976) defined six stages of moral development in children (Maccoby, 1980). First during preconventional morality, at approximately 2 to 7 years, the following are appropriate.

1 Obedience. Children have no real moral sense, but their behaviour can be shaped through rewards and sanctions.

2   Naive egoism. A child defines 'right' as something that works for them. There is no reference to other people in their decisions. They may appear to be able to meet other people's needs but it is only because the result is favourable to the child.

Then comes conventional morality, at approximately 2 to 11 years, when the following are appropriate.

3   Good girl/boy orientation. Children try to please, initially only in specific circumstances where they have learned what to do. Eventually this becomes more general as they learn what good girl/boy means.

4   Authority maintaining orientation. Moral ideas become generalised and children begin to obey rules not, as previously because a significant other requires it of them, but because of a sense of duty towards authority and to maintain the social order.

Finally there is postconventional morality, from the age of approximately 12 years onwards. Some people never reach this stage of moral development.

5   Contractual legalism. A sense of duty is still strong but issues of fairness and legality become more important than just maintaining the social order. Rules are seen as arbitrary things subject to possible, and sometimes desirable, change.

6   General principles of conscience. Moral ideas form part of an individual, coherent philosophy. Moral decisions take into account many variables and the individual can look beyond fairness and legality.

An understanding of the stages of moral development means that planning and interaction with young children can be contingent upon their developmental level. The ways in which a sense of right and wrong is communicated to young children can then be developmentally appropriate. It is evident from Kohlberg's stages of moral development that pre-school-aged children are beginning to become aware that their actions and attitudes affect other people, also that rules govern and shape our behaviour and that these rules need to be kept. These skills need to be developed and encouraged for children to begin to have an awareness of morality.

CASE STUDY

Early moral development

At the collage table Leon was making a fire engine. He had built the engine and was finishing it by sticking small pieces of red shiny paper on it. This meant that he needed the glue frequently. He had the glue for some time when another child, at the other side of the table asked if she could have the glue. Leon passed the glue to the girl and said 'Tell everyone that it's my turn next with the glue.' He then turned to the staff member and said 'I've been a good boy haven't I, I've shared?'

Leon had obviously learned that it is good to share. He obeys this rule when he passes the glue to another child. He does however make sure that the glue returns quickly to him by announcing that it is his turn next. He clearly wants to please the adult present at the activity as he draws her attention to something that he recognises will please her. It is evident from this that the motivation for his actions are external. The benefits to him are the approval of a significant other. The motivation for his action is that he wants to be seen to be a 'good boy' rather than the realisation that sharing and cooperation are necessary to the social order. In Kohlberg's stages of moral development he is at the stages of, obedience, naive egoism and good girl/boy orientation.

1 Explain why Leon is at the stages of obedience, naive egoism and good girl/boy orientation.
2 How could a childcare worker develop Leon's skills in this situation?
3 How could a childcare worker use this situation to develop an awareness of morality for the other children at the activity?

Pre-school-aged children are beginning to become aware that their actions and attitudes affect other people

GOOD PRACTICE

Evidence suggests that moral development is best facilitated by giving children the opportunity to understand principles and reasons rather than to teach specific actions that may be situationally dependent (Curtis, 1986). In this way children will come to an understanding of morality through interaction and not indoctrination.

At pre-school level children need to begin to understand the interdependence of people within society and, that for society to function successfully, we need to consider other people in our own actions and attitudes. Children, therefore, need the opportunity to feel what it is like to be someone else. As they begin to empathise with other people they can then take account of this in their own actions and attitudes.

Children also need to begin to understand rules and why they exist. Initially they will accept these rules because a significant other enforces them. However, eventually, as a child understands the reasons why they exist they will begin to internalise them as moral values.

Exploration of these issues needs to be appropriate to the child. Listed below are some ideas.

- Books. Through listening to stories children can experience a wide range of emotions. They can enter the experiences of another person as they begin to empathise with the characters in the story. They can become involved in a wider range of experiences than their own.
- Role play and dressing up. In a role-play or dressing-up situation children can feel, at first hand what it is like to be someone or something else. This is a developmentally appropriate way for children, who tend to be egocentric, to begin to understand things from another viewpoint.
- Puppets. Puppets also enable children to take on new and different roles. They have the added benefit of disguise for the child. Again, a child has to enter the experiences of another person to enable them to take on the role.

Imaginative play enables children to feel what it is like to be somebody or something else

- Games that involve a notion of fairness and regulation. The adult needs to take responsibility for the smooth running of the game by ensuring that:
  - turns are taken

- equal turns are given to each person
- people begin on a equal footing
- the rules are adhered to.

These notions of fairness and regulation need to be pointed out to children and an explanation given for what the adult is doing.

■ A structural framework of rules. Rules need to be kept to a minimum as too many won't be remembered. The rules must:
- express the values, expectations and ethos of an establishment
- be justifiable
- be understood by everyone within the establishment and by parents
- be consistently applied
- be modelled by staff members.

PROGRESS CHECK

1 What is morality?

2 Why might there be disagreement between people about what is right and what is wrong?

3 Why is morality closely linked with interpersonal skills?

4 What is social empathy and why is it important to the development of morality?

5 Explain Kohlberg's stages of moral development.

6 Why do childcare workers need to understand these stages of moral development?

7 What aspects of morality are young children beginning to become aware of?

8 Explain how moral development is best facilitated.

9 Give some examples of how to achieve moral development in a childcare setting.

KEY TERMS

You need to know what these words and phrases mean. Go back through the chapter and make sure that you understand:

conventional morality	preconventional morality
developmentally appropriate	rewards
ideal self	role models
independence	self concept
interpersonal skills	self esteem
morality	significant other
postconventional morality	

Further reading

Bruce, T., *Time To Play*, Hodder & Stoughton, London, 1991
Curtis, A., *A Curriculum for the Pre-school Child*, NFER-Nelson, 1986

6 LANGUAGE AND LITERACY

> **This chapter covers:**
> - An introduction to Language and Literacy in the pre-school curriculum
> - Developing talking and listening skills
> - Developing an appreciation of stories, rhymes and books
> - The pre-school curriculum and early writing and reading
> - Developing early writing
> - Developing early reading

An introduction to Language and Literacy in the pre-school curriculum

Language and Literacy are vital elements of the pre-school curriculum, being the basis of all later learning. Children up to the age of 5 are at a very important learning stage in their acquisition of language and literacy skills, for it is during this period that most children will learn to talk and begin to read and write. The pre-school curriculum is concerned with developing initial skills and concepts that enable children to successfully acquire these skills.

> *In small and large groups, children listen attentively and talk about their experiences. They use a growing vocabulary with increasing fluency to express thoughts and convey meaning to the listener. They listen and respond to stories, songs, nursery rhymes and poems. They make up their own stories and take part in role play with confidence.*
>
> *Children enjoy books and handle them carefully, understanding how they are organised. They know that words and pictures carry meaning and that, in English, print is read from left to right and top to bottom. They begin to associate sounds with patterns in rhymes, with syllables, and with words and letters. They recognise their own name and some familiar words. They recognise letters of the alphabet by shape and sound. In their writing they use pictures, symbols and familiar words and letters to communicate meaning, showing awareness of some of the different purposes of writing. They write their name with appropriate use of upper and lower case letters.*
>
> (Desirable Outcomes for Children's Learning, *DfEE with SCAA, 1996*)

CREATING A LITERATE ENVIRONMENT

Language and literacy are learned skills. They are acquired by children through interaction with their environment. The richer and more varied the environment the better the child's learning and understanding is likely to be. Therefore it is important that establishments that care for young children, who are developing these skills, create a literate environment.

We live in a literate world, that is a society that values reading and writing as important and necessary skills. Everyone, including children, is surrounded by the products of literacy, for example on billboards, food packets, road signs, bills and letters. Children also come into contact with the process of literacy, for example signing your name, taking down messages, writing shopping lists, reading directions, reading bus times, and so on. These experiences enable young children to become aware of the uses of literacy skills and of their importance. Children coming into a pre-school setting will, therefore, already have experience of the uses of language and literacy.

This literate environment needs to be evident within a pre-school setting. Children need to be surrounded by, and involved in creating a literate environment. Some suggestions are listed below.

- Label toy boxes – with both picture and word for the youngest children.
- Put up signs: 'to the toilet', 'to the playground', 'to the cloak room', 'to the kitchen', etc.

Labelling creates a literate environment

- Label displays.
- Label role play areas with appropriate signs and charts. Where appropriate provide menus, price lists, maps and instructions.
- Do the register with all the children together. Discuss why it is done and how you record their attendance.
- Make lists with the children when planning.
- Label children's work and discuss why you are labelling it.
- Point out and read signs, posters, labelling and instructions in the child's environment.

All lettering should be of a high standard. When labelling in English this includes:

- proper use of upper and lower case lettering
- correct spelling
- always writing from left to right in a straight line.

When labelling in other languages other rules may apply. It is, of course essential to ensure that labelling etc. in languages other than English is correctly written. Parents and the local community are valuable sources of information. Where this is not available some local education authorities provide a translation service.

Labelling in languages other than English reflects the linguistic diversity within society

PROGRESS CHECK

1 Why are language and literacy vital elements of the pre-school curriculum?
2 Outline an appropriate language and literacy pre-school curriculum.
3 Why is ours a literate world?
4 How can you create a literate environment in the pre-school setting?
5 What is important about the lettering displayed in the pre-school setting?
6 Why are these things particularly important for young children who are acquiring early literacy skills?

Developing talking and listening skills

Listening and talking are the earliest skills that a child acquires. Young children are very sensitive to language and eager to learn. We know that the quality of interaction that a child receives is directly linked to their language ability, and language ability has been shown to have a profound affect on all learning. To develop language successfully children need a rich, stimulating environment that provides the opportunity for experiences appropriate to their level of development. There are a number of factors that affect the quality of the language environment:

Talking with others is necessary for children to pick up language and to adjust and refine their language skills

- the presence of positive role models
- the opportunity for children to practice their language skills
- positive feedback to enable the children to pick up language and to adjust and refine their language skills.

GOOD PRACTICE IN TALKING WITH CHILDREN

People who work with young children need to adopt practices that contribute positively to children's language development.

Listed below are some important points to remember when talking with children, however, these are only practical suggestions, and a sensitivity towards individual children's needs, interests and developmental level is the basis of positive interaction.

- The tone of your voice. Does the tone of your voice convey warmth and an interest in the child?
- Your rate of speech How quickly do you speak? Do you speak at a pace that is appropriate to the child or children you are talking to?
- Listening. How do you show the child that you are listening? Eye contact and physically getting down to the child's level show that you are listening. Becoming involved in the conversation also indicates that you are listening.
- Waiting. Do you leave enough time for the child to respond? Young children may need time to formulate their responses. It is also important to remember that pauses and silences are part of conversation.
- Questions. How many questions do you ask? Too many may make a conversation feel like a question-and-answer session, especially if your response is 'That's right'. The type of question asked is also important. Closed questions that require a single word answer or a nod do not give children the opportunity to practice and develop their language skills. Open questions that have a range of possible answers allow children to practice their language skills and develop their ideas.
- Your personal contribution. It is important to contribute your own experience and/or opinions to the conversation. This demonstrates interest and involvement with the child.
- Diverse language experiences. You need to consider how much of your time is involved in management talk, conversation and chatting, explanation or playful talk. Children need experience of a wide range of language experiences to enable them to practice and refine their language skills.
- Developing thought. Good practice involves asking for and giving reasons and explanations when talking to children. Children need to be encouraged to give an account of what they are doing or have done and to make predictions in real and imaginary situations. In these ways their thoughts and ideas can be expressed and developed.
- Who do you talk to? All children need the opportunity to practice and develop their language. Good practice is to talk with all children, at some time, on an individual basis. It is the responsibility of the staff to ensure that this happens. There will be a range of developmental levels within every group of children and it is important that each child's needs are met. This may involve careful planning to

ensure that there is the time and opportunity for staff to focus on individual children.

CASE STUDY

Talking with children (1)

A day nursery decided to have a themed day. The theme was red. The staff wore red clothes and encouraged the children to do so. The activities set out were themed on red: red construction equipment, red dye in the water, red dough, different shades of red paint, red equipment in the home corner. Two staff members were given the task of ensuring that they made contact with each child individually at some point in the day. They intended to spend some time in conversation with each child and where and when appropriate discuss the day, the clothes, the activities etc.

The nursery nurses decided to divide the main group up and each work with a small group of children. They produced lists of the group and when they had found an opportunity to converse with a child, crossed the name off the list. By mid afternoon each had a few children they needed to seek out and converse with. In this way they ensured that all the children in the nursery had the opportunity to talk to an adult on a particular day about a particular subject. They were also able to make an assessment of each child's language development and whether they had a concept of the colour red. This then enabled them to plan further activities and experiences accordingly.

1 Why do you think it was important for the staff to ensure that they spoke to all the children?
2 Why do you think it would be easy to miss talking to some children in the day nursery?
3 How did the staff ensure that no children were missed out on this particular day?
4 How could this system of ensuring that all children are spoken to be built into the everyday routine in the nursery?
5 Where possible, observe a group of children. Which children are talked with? What kinds of language are used (management, chat, conversation, playful talk, explanation etc.)? How could the present practice be improved to ensure that all children receive rich and varied language experiences?

CASE STUDY

Talking with children (2)

From the themed day outlined in case 1 the staff in the nursery were able to identify a number of children whom they felt needed some small group language work and/or did not have a clear concept of the colour red. In their planning the staff chose these children, as a group, to work with a member of staff at group time. The aim of these sessions was to involve the children in listening and talking and, where needed, develop a concept of the colour red. Five sessions were planned.

Session 1 A group storytime using a story about the colour red was held. The staff had made up a story about a red balloon that flew away in the nursery and a child had to chase it. The story included many familiar places within the nursery. The nursery nurse told the children the story and then each child was asked to describe one of the places that the balloon had gone.

Session 2 Michael prepared a red balloon hunt. He placed the balloons around the nursery in the places that were in the story and the children had to find a balloon. Each child then described where they had found their balloon and, as a group, they made a list of the hiding places.

Session 3 The following day the children were asked to try to remember where all the red balloons had been hidden and ticked the hiding places off the list. When they had remembered and described all the places they did some paintings of the balloons.

Session 4 Michael brought the paintings to the group session and they all described what they had painted and discussed a suitable caption for each painting. The children were encouraged to describe and discuss their own and each others' paintings. Michael wrote the caption on the paintings with the children and they made the story into a book.

Taping is a good way of recording young children's stories

Session 5 The children were then encouraged to make up their own story about the adventures of the red balloon. This was done as a group with each child contributing an idea. The children taped their story to play to the whole group.

1 Why was it important that these children were targeted?
2 How did the nursery nurse encourage the children's language development?
3 How did the nursery nurse encourage development of the children's concept of red?
4 Refer to the section on developing talking and listening skills and describe in detail some of the ways in which the nursery nurse could interact with the children in a positive way.
5 How could these activities be followed up to consolidate the learning?
6 Read back through the case studies. Identify where learning from other curriculum areas is evident.
7 Why is this integrated approach developmentally appropriate for young children?

LISTENING

Although most people are born with the ability to listen and take it for granted, it is in fact quite a complex skill. Listening involves sifting out and selecting relevant information from all the incoming information. This skill is acquired and children need encouragement to achieve this. It is a particularly important skill as it enables children to make full use of the opportunities offered to them.

This skill of active listening demands good powers of concentration. A child needs to be able to attend and focus their attention on the task. Young children need the opportunity to acquire these skills.

GOOD PRACTICE IN DEVELOPING LISTENING SKILLS

Young children need to be encouraged to listen carefully and focus their attention. This requires adult and child interaction. It can be achieved across the nursery curriculum. Some ideas are listed below.

- Go through a story after having read it for the children to recall what they have heard.
- Ask the children to look out for a particular event or character in a story.
- Give simple instructions for the children to follow.
- Learn songs, rhymes and poems.
- Encourage children to play with sounds and words, for example:
  - rhyming words
  - sound bingo – listening for the same word
  - tongue twisters
  - whispering games
- Go on sound walks – focusing on what children can hear in a particular place.
- Model careful listening yourself.

Listening

A playgroup planned to visit a farm park. Before they went they did a lot of work on identifying animals and the sounds they make. As part of this the playgroup leader made a sound lotto game for the children to play. She made a tape of animal noises and a lotto set of animal pictures. The children had to listen to the tape and match the sound to an animal.

Before the activity was put out the tape was played to the children at storytime. A number of different activities were introduced to encourage the children to focus their attention on the sounds. They identified the animals and copied the sounds. They imitated the sounds for the others to identify. They described an animal and the children had to make the appropriate noise. In these ways the children achieved the aim of learning about animals and the sounds they make and also they had been encouraged to listen in an active rather than passive way.

1 Why is this a meaningful way for children to develop listening skills?
2 Outline the adult's role in this activity.

PROGRESS CHECK

1 Why is it important to talk with young children?
2 List and explain the aspects of good practice when talking with young children.
3 How can good practice in talking with young children be achieved within your workplace?
4 What is active listening?
5 Why is active listening important to children's learning?
6 Outline ways in which active listening can be achieved in a pre-school setting.

Developing an appreciation of stories, rhymes and books

Books, stories and rhymes are enjoyable for young children. A quiet, intimate and enjoyable story session with an adult creates a positive association for the child. This in turn helps to establish a habit of reading and listening to stories which will have many benefits for the child.

Books, stories and rhymes are an important part of creating a literate environment. Children need to have rich and varied language experiences and books stories and rhymes extend their experiences beyond everyday language. They provide an insight into worlds and experiences beyond the child's own experiences and, therefore, use language beyond the child's own experiences. Fantasy books provide children with imaginative and diverse experiences that require imaginative and diverse language. The greater a child's exposure to these different patterns in language the richer and more varied their own expressive (spoken) language is likely to be.

Through contact with books children begin to understand the uses and purposes of writing and reading. They gradually begin to understand that the squiggles on the page represent speech and that you can decode then to understand what they say. These are vital early reading and writing skills.

There are many ways of making a story/rhyme session varied and interesting. This not only maintains young children's interest but provides a wide variety of language experiences. Stories can be read from a book, made up and told to the children, told through the use of props and/or puppets, acted out or made up with the children, encouraging them to suggest what happened next.

Similarly, rhymes and poems may be known or made up by both staff and children. They may be rhyming couplets or stories in a poem format such as 'The Owl and the Pussycat'. Rhymes and poems in languages other than English can be introduced. Children can learn some Makaton signing, a simplified sign language used in conjunction with speech, to accompany the rhymes and poems. A useful video for this purpose is Dave Benson Phillips' 'Makaton Nursery Rhymes' video (Polygram).

CASE STUDY

Preparing for a theatre visit

A theatre group was going to visit a nursery to do a performance of 'Goldilocks and the Three Bears'. The theatre group encouraged the children to be actively involved in the performance, so the staff wanted to make the children aware of the story before the theatre group came so that they could participate in the performance. Initially, the staff member told the story to the whole group.

The following day the staff member used a treasure chest as a prop. In it she had put a wig, hats, bowls, spoons and pillows. As she told the story she produced the props from the treasure chest, much to the children's delight. She them retold the story encouraging the children to select the appropriate prop at the appropriate point in the story.

The props were then put into the role play area , which was the three bears' house, so that the children could play with them.

When the theatre company did their performance the children were able to become fully involved in the experience as they knew the story. They were able to sequence the events, anticipate what came next, join in the storytelling and direct the cast. All this enhanced the children's enjoyment of the occasion. It formed a positive association with stories and theatre which is valuable for children's language development and, therefore, later learning.

GOOD PRACTICE FOR STORYTIME

Storytime needs to be considered as carefully as any other activity. The following are points to consider for storytime sessions with individuals and with groups.

■ The choice of book: is it developmentally appropriate? (See page 111).

Books are a powerful way of influencing children's views about the society they live in. Books for children must, therefore, reflect positive images of all sections of society in both the text and the illustrations.

0–3
- Picture books are appropriate for this age range, especially for children under 1 year.
- Where there is text it needs to be limited, especially for children aged 0–1.
- The pictures need to have bright colours and bold shapes.
- The pictures need little detail.
- The images need to be simplified so that they are easily identified – the most obvious features stressed.
- Children enjoy familiar themes, for example families, animals.
- The complexity of pictures and text can be increased for children aged 2+.
- The context of the story time is as important as the book itself; the cosy, close and intimate time gives children a positive association with books and reading.

3–5
- Repetition is important – for language development and for the enjoyment of the sound and rhythm of language.
- Books need to be reasonably short, to match children's concentration span.
- Books need minimum language with plenty of pictures that relate to the text.
- Popular themes are still everyday objects and occurrences.

5–7
- A clearly identifiable story and setting are important.
- Children's wider interests, experiences and imagination should be reflected in themes.
- The characters can be developed through the story.
- Language usage can be richer – playing with rhyme and rhythm, the introduction of new vocabulary and the use of repetition for dramatic effect.

3–7
- Illustrations still need to be bold, bright and eye-catching but can be more detailed and have more meaning than pure recognition.
- Sequenced stories become popular – with a beginning, middle and end.
- The storyline needs to be easy to follow with a limited number of characters.
- Repetition is important so that the reader or listener can become involved in the text.
- Animated objects are popular – children can enter into the fantasy.
- Children enjoy humour in stories, but it needs to be obvious humour, not puns or sarcasm.

Guidelines for choosing books for young children

- Check that the book portrays positive images of all societal groups and individuals in both the storyline and the pictures.
- Are there any props that could enhance the story, such as puppets, a treasure chest, props, a storyboard or music?
- Do you know the story well enough to make these judgements and to tell the story in an appropriate way?
- Allow the children to see the pages as you read the book.
- Point to the words as you read, demonstrating left to right tracking and identifying individual words as you say them. This will help children begin to develop aural reading and writing skills.
- Tell the story enthusiastically. Children will pick up on your enthusiasm. It is best to have read the story beforehand so that you can concentrate on your storytelling rather than following the text.

Storytime

- Talk about the story when you have finished reading it through. It is advisable to read the story through initially, without interruption, to maintain the flow of the storyline. Constant interruptions may mean that the children lose the sense of the story. After this you could encourage the children to:

- retell the story sequencing the events
- comment on the characters and/or events
- recognise similarities within their own experiences
- develop the storyline with, 'What could happen next?' or 'What if?' questions
- join in rhymes, songs and poems that develop the themes introduced in the story
- retell the story using puppets and/or props.

PROGRESS CHECK

1 Why is a positive attitude towards books, stories and rhymes important for young children?

2 How can books extend children's language experiences?

3 Describe how storytime can be made varied and interesting.

4 Describe how you can vary children's experiences with rhymes and poems.

5 Why is careful planning essential to good storytelling?

6 List and explain what you need to consider before you tell children a story.

The pre-school curriculum and early writing and reading

The pre-school curriculum is concerned with developing a range of skills and concepts that enable children to successfully learn to read and to write. Both reading and writing are fundamental to all later learning. It is, therefore, essential that these early skills and concepts are well established as they form a foundation for later learning. It is important to understand how children are taught to read and to write so that early learning can be based upon the same techniques, and this section will outline how this is achieved. However, most pre-school-aged children are not yet intellectually or physically mature enough to begin reading and writing. The focus in the pre-school curriculum should, therefore, be the development and consolidation of necessary early skills and concepts.

Adult interaction with children is essential in developing these skills and concepts. The only way that children have access to this sort of information is through interested and knowledgeable adults. A lot of learning is done informally at home and in a pre-school setting but writing and reading are some of the skills that cannot be acquired informally. Therefore, an adult within a pre-school setting must pay particular attention to providing activities and experiences that develop these necessary skills.

The adult must carefully plan the activities based on an assessment of the children's needs and abilities. This requires intimate knowledge of each individual child. Once the child is engaged in the activity the adult needs to interact with the child, introducing concepts, providing explanations and discussing and describing what is happening. The adult must ensure that the activity is appropriate to each child's development and adapt their interaction as necessary. Finally the adult must monitor the child's progress during the activity to ensure that future planning is appropriate.

Before any activities are planned specifically to develop early reading and writing there are certain skills that children need:

- visual discrimination – the ability to distinguish one thing from another by sight
- auditory discrimination – the ability to distinguish one sound from another
- the ability to sequence – both reading and writing rely upon appropriate sequencing of letters and words
- the ability to symbolise – using one item to represent another. Reading and writing are symbolic representations of speech – the squiggles that are written down and decoded to be read represent the spoken word. This ability to use things representationally begins initially in a child's play. They begin to use one item to represent another, for example a doll becomes a baby, a box becomes a boat, blue plastic sheeting becomes a river. Once this skill is acquired it is transferable, in this case to reading and writing, and squiggles written on a page can be used to represent speech.

Children need activities that develop these skills. Many of the activities listed below develop a number of these skills. Children need time to develop and to consolidate their skills through a wide range of play activities. Some ideas for play activities are:

- sorting and matching toys and games
- sequencing activities – threading, construction equipment, drawing and painting, weaving, creating patterns in sand, collage
- stories, songs, rhymes and poems – both spoken and role played – these have sequences and develop powers of auditory discrimination
- ring games – again these have a sequence and develop powers of auditory discrimination
- role play and dressing up
- large and small construction toys
- experience with paper and writing equipment.

As reading and writing are closely linked many of the skills and concepts apply equally to both areas. For ease of explanation they are separated here, however, development of these skills in a pre-school setting should always be integrated.

It is important to remember that some other languages have different conventions and that there may be children who are learning two or more systems of reading and writing. It is important the people who work with bilingual or multilingual children are aware of what the child is learning at home and what the similarities and differences are between the child's home language and English. (For example, is the alphabet different to English? What are the writing conventions?) The curriculum can then be made appropriate to the individual child. The sheer volume of information that a bilingual or multilingual child has to learn may mean that their acquisition of these skills may be slightly slower initially, but all the evidence suggests that, where there is this initial delay, it is made up very quickly.

PROGRESS CHECK

1 What is the aim of the pre-school early writing and reading curriculum?

2 Why are these early writing and reading skills vital?

3 Why is adult interaction necessary to children's learning?

4 Outline the skills that young children need to have before specific writing and reading activities are planned.

5 Identify activities within the workplace that develop these skills.

6 Why should early writing and reading skills be integrated?

7 Describe ways in which childcare workers can be sensitive to the needs of bilingual children.

Developing early writing

Writing is a skill that brings together a complex range of physical skills and cognitive understanding. Young children need to acquire these skills and concepts and to practice and refine them throughout the pre-school years. The aim of the pre-school curriculum is therefore to provide the opportunity for acquisition and practice of the skills and concepts that will enable a child to successfully learn to write.

GOOD PRACTICE IN DEVELOPING EARLY WRITING

Skills and concepts that young children need to develop and to consolidate include:
- a concept of the purposes of writing
- an understanding of writing conventions
- fine motor skills needed for writing
- recognition of alphabet sounds
- recognition of patterns that form familiar words.

A concept of the purposes of writing

Children need to understand what writing is and why and how it is used. Children then have a realistic context in which to place their learning.

Most children will come to the pre-school setting with experience of when writing is used, for example writing lists, signing names, labelling and writing letters notes and cards. The initial step in young children's learning is to make them aware of these instances in their everyday experiences and to explain the reasons why we write things down, for example, writing names on paintings so that we know whose they are either to display or to take home. This can be achieved by informally pointing out the occurrences of writing in their everyday lives.

Once children understand this, it can be extended to role play: a café where they take orders, a post office where they address envelopes or a doctor's surgery where they write out prescriptions. If this play is carefully planned and structured and adults are involved when appropriate, these play experiences will further enable a child to become aware of the reasons why writing is necessary. Children who have acquired this concept of writing may begin to make marks on a page. These marks represent speech and children will often tell you what they say. This is sometimes called emergent or early writing.

Other opportunities can be used to draw children's awareness to the necessity for writing. A shopping trip may require a shopping list, an outing may require a list of

Prices
envelopes ... 10p
stamps 20p
postcards . 5p
tape 50p
glue 50p
string 20p

Children can develop an awareness of the purposes of writing through role play

things to take and registration requires a list of names. These opportunities can also be used to point out the conventions in writing English.

CASE STUDY

Emergent writing

A collage activity on shiny things was planned. The nursery nurse introduced the activity with a treasure chest. The children discussed what 'shiny' looked like and identified some shiny paper. They then sorted the shiny pieces of paper from the treasure chest. The children did the activity and the nursery nurse mounted the work. Emily wanted to discuss her picture. She described how she had used the shiny paper to make a puddle so that you could see a tree reflected in it. She wanted to write this down so that people would know what she had done. She made a series of marks on the paper consisting of some recognisable letters and other shapes. She told the nursery nurse that it said, 'a puddle with a tree in it'. The nursery nurse wrote out a caption and put it up with the work in the display.

Emily demonstrated that she understood one of the purposes of writing. She had experience of captions on displays and recognised that they convey meaning, they tell people what the picture is. She also demonstrated that she had a concept of writing – the recording of speech through squiggles on a page. She had a grasp of some letters and this was evident in her 'writing'. This skill was yet to be refined but the initial concept was there, her writing skills were emerging.

1 What concepts had Emily understood?
2 How did Emily demonstrate that she had these concepts?
3 How did the nursery nurse provide the opportunity for her to practice this skill?

Opportunities for demonstrating reading and writing conventions occur across the nursery curriculum

An understanding of English writing conventions

Writing conventions in English are:

- left to right orientation
- top to bottom orientation
- standardised spelling that reflects sounds (phonics) and/or shape (look and say) with upper and lower case lettering
- standardised punctuation that makes the text make sense
- standardised grammar

  The following are ways in which learning the conventions can be achieved.

- Pointing to the text when reading a book to children. This will demonstrate going from left to right and top to bottom.

- Asking children and/or drawing children's attention to where you start when you write something down. An important concept is that having finished one line you go back to the beginning of another. This can also be pointed out to children as you write.
- Highlighting the fact that their name is always written in the same way, and encouraging children to recognise their name which may at first be recognition of the initial letter. This can be achieved by familiarity with the name through labelling cloakroom pegs, children's own work boxes and creative work, for example.
- Making children aware of the standard spelling in familiar names, signs and packaging. Children will be able to recognise a wide range of words and logos within their environment. These may be incorporated in role play situations such as a shop or a garage.
- Pointing out obvious punctuation marks in text such as question marks.

CASE STUDY

Writing conventions

On a trip to a local art gallery the staff of a playgroup took a series of photographs. The following day the children looked at the photographs and talked about the trip. They decided to make a big book about the trip as a book for their book corner and to show to the parents who had not been able to come with them.

The children sorted and ordered the photographs to reflect the pattern of the day. They then stuck one on each page. Each photograph was then discussed and the children decided what to write on each page. As the children decided upon a suitable caption the play leader wrote it on the page. Initially she talked through what she was doing, beginning on the left and returning to the left-hand side of the paper at the beginning of each line, saying the sounds of the letters, pointing out full stops and question marks and talking about where a capital letter was needed. After a few pages she began to ask the children questions.

- Where she should start?
- What happens when she has finished a line?
- What should she put at the beginning of someone's name?
- Can anyone remember what this dot is for?
- How do you know that it is a question when something is written down?
- Can anyone recognise any sounds or letters?

When the book was finished, the nursery nurse showed it to all the children at storytime. One child wanted to show the others a question mark. He explained that it showed that a question had been written down. This prompted a discussion about the other writing conventions. The nursery nurse was able to go over the writing conventions that she had used in the book and consolidate the work done earlier.

In this way the adult can introduce writing conventions to children in a meaningful context. The children could see the necessity for writing and be introduced to how this can be achieved when writing English.

1 Why is this a meaningful context in which to introduce writing conventions?
2 Identify the good practice shown by this play leader.
3 How could this activity be extended to further consolidate the children's learning?

A visit to an art gallery is a starting point for making a class book

Fine motor skills needed for writing

Writing requires controlled manipulation of writing implements. Young children need to acquire these fine motor skills. Development of these skills is partially maturational and partly to do with practice. Throughout the pre-school years most children's maturation will be appropriate to the development of the necessary fine motor skills. Alongside this children need many opportunities to practice and refine these fine motor skills. This can be achieved through a wide range of activities, for example threading, weaving, clay and dough modelling, sorting, small construction and ball games which all develop fine motor coordination.

Children also need a wide range of experience with drawing and writing implements. The majority of these pre-school experiences should be free exploration and practice. During this stage of development children need to be encouraged to hold the implements correctly. For most children it will be towards the end of pre-school

Threading activities contribute to the development of fine motor skills

that they progress to any form of copywriting. It is important to be aware that many schools now teach children to join their writing up from the outset.

Copywriting involves a child following patterns, aiming to make intentional marks that begin to represent standardised writing. This eventually will be refined into copying their name. Copywriting needs to be introduced slowly as an interesting activity that has a focus other than drawing a line! The following are examples.

1 An activity that involves following a simple undulating line, for example tracing the bee's pathway to the hive; tracing the pattern on a hot air balloon.
2 Once this skill is established with simple patterns, more complex writing patterns can be introduced perhaps into the same activities.
3 From here children can continue writing patterns beyond what has been given, for example finish designing a patterned jumper; matching pairs by drawing a particular pattern.
4 Throughout this time children may be attempting to copy their name and there is no reason to discourage this. However, most children will find it difficult to achieve copywriting their name successfully until they have the fine motor skills that come from the activities above. By the end of pre-school many children will be able to copywrite their name.

It is important that this is not introduced too early. A child needs to have a good chance of succeeding, as consistent failure is likely to produce a negative association with writing. As writing is fundamental to the learning process children need to feel that they can be successful at it.

Recognition of alphabet sounds

Pre-school children need to begin to recognise sounds that build words. This is the phonic (sound) alphabet. Initially this will be the ability to say the sounds. Only later will they associate a sound with the written letter. The aim is to make children aware of the sounds and where they occur within a meaningful context. For pre-school-aged children this means that this learning must be done in ways that are familiar and concrete. Once children are able to hear the difference between sounds they need to be able to make an immediate link between a sound heard and an item that they can see and/or feel.

Enabling children to hear the differences between sounds can be achieved through:

- making children aware of sounds around them and getting them to listen carefully, for example getting children to close their eyes and listening for a few seconds and telling you what they can hear
- differentiating between familiar sounds, for example animal noises
- songs and rhymes that are based on repetitive sounds
- stories that emphasis particular sounds
- making up short sentences and captions that emphasise a particular sound.

Once children are able to differentiate between sounds they need to begin to link this with concrete examples of words that begin with a particular sound

Once children are able to differentiate some sounds they need to begin to link this with concrete examples of words that begin with a particular sound. This can be achieved through:

- sound books and displays – a collection of items that begin with a particular sound. To make this meaningful to children they must be involved in collecting the items and pictures
- pointing out and sounding initial letters familiar to them – the first letter of their name
- sound walks where children have to look for things beginning with a particular sound
- games where clues are given as sounds such as feely bags 'Can you feel something beginning with "s"?'; I Spy: a treasure hunt where treasure found begins with a particular sound.

Recognition of patterns that form familiar words

As well as sounding out words, words can be learned through a look-and-say approach: that is recognition of the patterns that form the words. It is also important to realise that the phonic alphabet is only suitable for some words, other words need to be recognised by their pattern and shape e.g. dough, bicycle, climbing frame. Regular and meaningful exposure to these words will enable children to recognise the patterns that form these words.

At a pre-school level this can be achieved through appropriate labelling that is pointed out to the children, for example labelling the appropriate box 'Dough tools', children will eventually associate this pattern of shapes (letters) with the item in the box.

Developing early reading

As with writing the aim in a pre-school setting is to develop a range of concepts and skills that will enable a child to successfully learn to read. Many of these skills and concepts are the same as for writing and development of them can be integrated. Again, as with writing, the context in which they are introduced must be meaningful to the child.

Teachers use a number of different approaches to teaching children to read. The combination used must be appropriate to each individual child. No single system should be used exclusively as some children adapt better to one system rather than another. An understanding of these approaches is useful to pre-school workers who are concerned with developing early reading skills. However, the stress in the pre-school setting should be establishing a good foundation for later learning and not on teaching children to read.

Teaching children to read

- Phonics: using sounds and sound combinations to build words. Children will 'sound out' a word when they read it.
- Look and say: children learn to recognise the pattern and shape of a word. All

children will need this skill sometimes as it is necessary for words that cannot be sounded out. However, some children use this approach most of the time.

■ Reading schemes: these are graded books, specially written to teach children to read, that have carefully structured language. Words are gradually introduced and the language is repetitive. They often have a familiar context such as recognisable characters. The children become familiar with the context and characters and begin to recognise the accompanying words. The structure of reading schemes is the introduction of new words into known text accompanied by appropriate pictures.

■ Real books: this method uses children's books to teach children to read. Some teachers allow children free choice of books, others grade the books. Where grading is done the books are banded and coded according to their language difficulty. Children select books within a band. Because these books are written as stories for children rather than to teach them to read this system has a broader language content and for this reason some teachers prefer it.

Good practice in developing early reading

Skills and concepts the children need to develop and to consolidate include:

■ an understanding of the purposes of reading
■ an understanding of reading conventions
■ recognition of the phonic alphabet
■ recognition of patterns that form familiar words.

An understanding of the purposes of reading

Children need to understand what reading is and when and how it is part of life. This gives children a meaningful context in which to place their learning. This concept of the purpose of reading is the first step towards an understanding of their need to acquire this skill. As with writing, many children will come to the pre-school setting with experience of when and how reading is used in society, for example stories read to them, reading packaging in shops, reading bus timetables, reading the newspaper and reading letters. These and other instances need to be highlighted to the children.

   In a pre-school setting this can be achieved through various ways.

■ Through role play, for example in a supermarket role play area where children need to read the packaging, shopping lists and prices.

■ Making children aware of when you are reading to demonstrate the necessity for it, for example reading out names on children's work when handing it out, marking the register, reading notes from parents/carers and reading letters to send home.

■ Labelling for information so that children need to read what is in a particular box, where to hang their coat, who did the painting on the wall or which drink is theirs, and so on.

■ Getting children to tell you a story and writing it down to make a class book that can be put into the reading area. Children can then 'read' the story to one another.

■ Making children aware when you are reading to them rather than telling them something, for example stories, messages and instructions.

A concept of the purposes of reading is important for young children

It is important to be aware that encouraging children's awareness of reading and its purposes is more prominent in some families than in others. Children will come to the pre-school setting with different experiences and abilities. The need for a differentiated curriculum based on clear assessment of individual children's abilities and experiences is, therefore, vital.

CASE STUDY

Shopping for the nursery pets

A number of things needed to be bought for the nursery's pet rabbit. A group of children and a playworker discussed what was needed and wrote a shopping list. At the shop the playworker read the list to the children as a reminder of what was needed and they walked around the shop together looking for the items. When they found an item, the playworker read the label to the children to make sure that it was the right thing. Before they went to the cash desk they read back through the list to check that they had got everything that they needed. The playworker encouraged the children to identify the items in the trolley and to read what was inside the package to check it against the list. On their return to the nursery they cleaned the rabbit out and fed him. Again the playworker encouraged the children to read the labels on the shopping to identify the items that they needed.

This was a simple and straightforward way to demonstrate to children why it is necessary to be able to read. The playworker achieved this through constant reference to the list, by focusing on reading the labels in the shop and by encouraging the children to become involved in reading the labels.

1 Why was this a meaningful context in which to introduce this concept?
2 How did the playworker demonstrate the need for reading?
3 Why was it important to encourage the children to get involved in reading the labels?
4 List some other ways in which young children can learn about the purposes of reading.

An understanding of English reading conventions
As with writing these include:
- left to right orientation – including how books are organised
- top to bottom orientation
- standardised spelling that reflects sounds (phonics) or the pattern and shape of a word (look and say)
- standardised punctuation that makes the text make sense
- standardised grammar.
  These can be achieved through various means.
- Always tracing the text with your finger, this demonstrates left to right and top to bottom orientation. Big, class-size books are useful for this.

Tracing the text with your finger demonstrates left to right and top to bottom orientation

- Showing children where you begin reading a book. This orientates children to the organisation of a book.
- Drawing children's attention to the fact that words are always written in the same way, for example their name is always written with the same letters in the same order.
- Use of correct punctuation and grammar in all writing.
- Identifying appropriate punctuation when reading to children.

Recognition of alphabet sounds

As with writing one of the skills required in order to read is the use of sounds to build words. Children need to learn the phonic alphabet. The aim is make children aware of the sounds and where they occur within a meaningful context. Therefore, the learning needs to be done in ways that are concrete and familiar to young children. Once children can differentiate between sounds they need to begin to make links between a sound and an item that they can see or feel. Interaction with an adult who is sensitive to the individual child's level of development is essential in the development of this skill.

The phonic alphabet can be learned through:
- rhymes, songs and stories that emphasise a particular sound
- games where children use initial sounds such as sound lotto, I spy and a feely box
- sound walks identifying items that begin with a particular sound
- collections of items and displays that begin with a particular sound, labelled with the appropriate word. These displays and their labelling need to be drawn to the children's attention. In this way children can 'read' the words associated with the item.

CASE STUDY

Learning the sound 'p'

A childcare worker planned a day focusing on the sound 'p'. He began with the whole group together and they looked at a collection of things that all began with the sound 'p'. They wrote out a label for each item and began a display, 'Things that begin with p'. They practised saying the sound and tried to learn the first line of the tongue twister, 'Peter Piper picked a peck of pickled peppercorn'.

The childcare worker then asked the children to look out for things during the day, helped by the staff, that began with the sound 'p'. When they found something they could bring it to him, and he would make a label to add to the display.

At storytime towards the end of the day the children looked at the display together. They identified the items and confirmed that their initial sound was 'p'. They also practised 'Peter Piper'.

The display was left for a week and children encouraged to add to it and to look at the additions that other children had made. Each time the children came together as a group the staff discussed changes in it and used it for activities to consolidate the learning. This included:

- a feely box for the children to identify an item
- adding items that did not begin with 'p' for the children to spot
- describing items without saying their name for the others to guess
- Kim's game – setting out a number of items and then removing one for the others to see if they could remember what was missing
- shopping lists – each person adding an item from the display to a shopping list and the next child having to say the whole list before adding their own item. For young children the items need to be seen and ordered.

1 How did the childcare worker get the children involved in this display?
2 Why is the children's involvement important?
3 Why was it important to keep the children's interest in the display?
4 How was maintaining the children's interest achieved?
5 How could the staff monitor the children's learning to ensure that all the children were developing this concept?

A display of things that begin with the sound 'p'

Recognition of patterns that form familiar words

At pre-school level this can be achieved through appropriate labelling which is drawn to the children's attention. In this way children can begin to associate a particular pattern of letters with a particular word and build up their sight vocabulary.

Recognition of letters

Samina, a four-year-old in a playgroup approached a playworker to say that she was looking for the sand play equipment and could not find the box. The playworker showed her where the box was and explained that all the boxes had a label on them that told you what was in them. She pointed out that the first letter of the label 'Sand play equipment' was the same as the first letter of 'Samina.' The following day Samina called the playworker over, she showed her the box and said, 'This is the sand toy box, I know because it's in my name.'

This demonstrates Samina's developing ability to recognise letters that form words. She is aware that what she is looking for is the familiar 's' as an initial letter. Eventually through contact with this pattern of letters ('sand play equipment') she will begin to recognise the pattern and to read it. This development of a 'look and say' vocabulary requires regular exposure to the words. Labelling in a pre-school setting, that requires the children to participate in recognition of the label, is a way of achieving this.

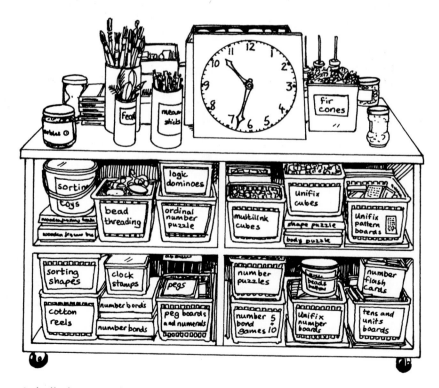

Labelled storage boxes help children to recognise patterns of letters that form familiar words

PROGRESS CHECK

1 What are the early writing and reading skills and concepts that young children need to acquire?

2 What is a concept of the purposes of writing and reading and why is it an important concept for young children to acquire?

3 How can this be achieved in a pre-school setting?

4 List the English writing and reading conventions.

5 How can these conventions be introduced to young children in a developmentally appropriate way?

6 How can children be encouraged to recognise alphabet sounds?

7 Why is labelling important in developing a child's look-and-say vocabulary?

KEY TERMS

You need to know what these words and phrases mean. Go back through the chapter and make sure that you understand:

ability to symbolise
auditory discrimination
developmentally appropriate
emergent writing
fine motor skills
interaction
left to right orientation
literate environment
look and say
phonics

positive feedback
positive role models
processes of literacy
products of literacy
reading schemes
real books
top to bottom orientation
visual discrimination
writing and reading conventions

---

7 *MATHEMATICS*

This chapter covers:
- **Understanding the breadth of pre-school maths**
- **Understanding and developing mathematical language**
- **Understanding counting and pre-school number**
- **Understanding and developing other areas of pre-school maths**
- **Promoting pre-school maths**
- **Further reading**

This important area of the pre-school curriculum covers children's mathematical understanding, particularly numeracy. Opportunities to develop mathematical skills should be provided through the practical activities that are part of any pre-school programme. Staff need to introduce mathematical language appropriately and to emphasise mathematical concepts.

> *Children use mathematical language, such as circle, in front of, bigger than and more, to describe shape, position, size and quantity. They recognise and recreate patterns. They are familiar with number rhymes, songs, stories, counting games and activities. They compare, sort, match, order, sequence and count using everyday objects. They recognise and use numbers to 10 and are familiar with larger numbers from their everyday lives. They begin to use their developing mathematical understanding to solve practical problems. Through practical activities children understand and record numbers, begin to show awareness of number operations, such as addition and subtraction, and begin to use the language involved.*
>
> (Desirable Outcomes for Children's Learning, *DfEE with SCAA, 1996*)

Understanding the breadth of pre-school maths

Maths is a part of everyday life and children's mathematical learning begins as soon as they start to become involved in their environment. Many of the child's everyday experiences have a mathematical component in them. For example, getting dressed involves sequencing (which order to put clothes on), matching (finding a pair of socks or shoes), sorting (putting on your own clothes and not your baby brother's). Pouring breakfast juice into a cup needs skills in estimating and an awareness of full or not full and choosing a teddy to fit into the pushchair may require a decision involving bigger or smaller. Children are surrounded by experiences that contribute to their mathematical understanding long before their formal schooling in the subject begins. The pre-school years provide an ideal opportunity for children to develop positive attitudes towards maths. They need to be supported by adults who are confident and aware of opportunities to explore and extend mathematical knowledge practically.

Pre-school maths is much more than number and computation. The setting should provide opportunities for children to be introduced to the breadth of maths in ways that match their developmental ability to process information. This will provide a firm foundation for later mathematical education.

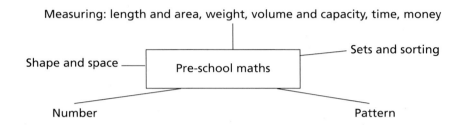

Maths in the pre-school setting is approached most effectively through practical activities. These are provided so that the children have an opportunity to meet and develop mathematical concepts through concrete experiences. Much of what children experience in any pre-school activity will involve an element of maths. This may be something that is planned, for example measuring sunflowers to find out which is tallest or it may arise incidentally perhaps when a child distributing birthday sweets discovers that they run out before everyone has had one. The childcare worker needs to be aware of the mathematical potential of any situation and be prepared to develop this through interactions with the children. The skilful adult observes the children and intervenes at the appropriate moment, listening and questioning, thus emphasising and consolidating the experience and giving children an opportunity to build on their experiences.

GOOD PRACTICE

Maths for pre-school children needs to be approached through practical activities guided by adults who are aware of the learning potential of the activity. Children who 'do' maths through firsthand experience are most likely to develop confidence and understanding in the subject.

CASE STUDY

A teddy bears' picnic

A group of children at nursery were involved in planning for a teddy bears' picnic including preparing the food. With the nursery nurse they decided on what they would need to buy and then planned a trip to the supermarket. This meant that the children had to select items from the shelves, making sure that they had the right ingredients. At the checkout they were helped to count out the money to pay, and pick up the change.

The children put the shopping in the bags, making sure that each bag was easy to carry. Back at the nursery, they unpacked the bags and checked that they had bought everything that they needed. One child expressed interest in the receipt and checked the price of everything they had bought. They then got on with preparing for the picnic by making sandwiches, decorating biscuits and setting out cups, plates and jugs of squash. The children were supported and encouraged by the nursery nurse throughout these preparations. She ensured that the activity went smoothly, that individual children were able to participate and that the learning potential of the activity was maximised by her skilful intervention in commenting and questioning.

This activity offered a great deal to the children across all areas of the curriculum, including meeting and using mathematical concepts in a context that is meaningful. The following maths experiences were provided through this activity:

- estimating – how much food to buy for the number of children at the party
- size – choosing size of packets of biscuits, loaves, jam
- money – paying at the checkout, recognising coins, notation of money, counting
- weight – balancing shopping bags evenly

Every day activities are rich in their potential for mathematics

- shape – fitting packets into shopping bags, cutting sandwiches into squares, triangles
- fractions – cutting sandwiches into halves, then quarters
- number – counting at supermarket, matching number of cups, plates to number of children
- pattern – decorating biscuits, repeating the pattern
- capacity – filling jugs, filling cups from jugs.

1 Why was this a successful activity?
2 How can the adult extend the children's learning in this kind of situation
3 What needs to be considered when planning this kind of activity?

PROGRESS CHECK

1 How should pre-school maths be approached?
2 Outline the role of the adult in providing for pre-school maths.
3 What does pre-school maths cover?
4 Why is it vital to promote positive attitudes to maths in the early years?

Understanding and developing mathematical language

Introducing children to mathematical language is an important aspect of this subject in the pre-school years. Staff need to plan for opportunities that allow children to meet mathematical language in the meaningful context of their everyday activities. Mathematical language is precise and specific and children may have difficulties in understanding and applying it. It will be necessary to explain, repeat and reinforce in order to consolidate understanding. The adult can best do this, both by observing children at play and introducing mathematical terminology as opportunities arise, as well as by structuring activities that are designed primarily to introduce or reinforce these terms. It should be remembered that children's use of a mathematical term does not necessarily guarantee understanding of the mathematical concept. Young children's understanding of these concepts is deeply embedded in experience: the concept cannot be grasped in isolation from the experience merely through the language. Young children will often misuse terms as they come to grips with both the concept and the words used to describe it. The pre-school worker needs to respond with sensitivity to these mistakes and use them to develop the child's understanding without undermining confidence.

CASE STUDY

Is it full?

A small group of three-year-olds were playing at the water tray alongside the nursery nurse. A large variety of buckets and cups and containers was provided and the children were enjoying filling, emptying and generally watching the water flow. The nursery nurse listened to the children, made suggestions and joined in the play. The children were using the words 'full' and 'empty' but inaccurately. To them, 'full' meant anything containing quite a lot of water and 'empty' was anything less than this. Their understanding was developing but the concepts of full and empty were, at this stage, imperfectly understood. The nursery nurse then started to fill her containers accompanying this by saying that this was full 'right up to the top and there's no more room'. As she emptied them out she commented that the water was all gone and that the beaker was empty. She then encouraged the children to carry on filling and emptying accompanying their efforts with the same kind of phrases, making sure that the containers were really 'full' and 'empty' this time.

1 Why intervene in this case?
2 In what ways was this intervention successful?
3 How could these children's understanding of the concept of full and empty be further developed?
4 Think of other examples that might indicate misunderstandings. What strategies could be used?

Many mathematical concepts rely on comparison. Plenty of opportunities will arise in the daily routine to introduce these ideas, often during group time, when the pre-school worker can structure the discussion around whether there are more girls than boys or more tables than easels, for example. Children will soon become involved in conversations around who is taller, smaller or older (comparatives) and this can be extended into introducing superlatives describing the group – tallest, smallest, oldest. The pre-school worker should emphasise the correct terms and encourage accuracy in the children's descriptions, for example the skipping rope is long, the shelf is narrow, her skirt is short, rather than rely on the more limited 'big' and 'little' that children might use.

GOOD PRACTICE

Mathematical terms can be difficult for children to understand. They need to be introduced alongside concrete experiences and reinforced when opportunities arise. Pre-school workers need to be aware of this and respond accordingly, ensuring that they use terms appropriately.

PROGRESS CHECK

1 Why is mathematical terminology sometimes difficult for children to grasp?
2 How can children's use of mathematical language be developed?
3 What can the pre-school worker do to consolidate children's understanding of mathematical language?

Understanding counting and pre-school number

Many pre-school children can recite numbers up to ten or twenty and beyond. This does not mean that they are competent in counting yet but that they know the words for numbers and their order. Counting is a complex process that requires application of the following principles.

- There must be one number-word for each item counted. This is known as the one-to-one principle and is crucial to counting.
- The process can be applied universally. It is the same process, whatever it is that you are counting.
- There must be a repeatable order to the number-words e.g. four will always come before five and after three.
- The number of the last item counted gives the cardinal value of the set.
- Where you start or where you finish makes no difference to the cardinal value of the set if the one-to-one principle is followed.

There is a great deal to grasp here, and observation of children in activities that involve counting will give childcare workers an indication of what is already known as well as what still needs to be accomplished.

CASE STUDY

Counting to ten?
Rita, aged three, was playing with a puzzle that had six lift-out pieces. The pieces were emptied out and she was counting the spaces going from left to right and touching each gap as she repeated the number. However, she carried on counting and reached ten, despite having run out of spaces, tapping the final space until she got to ten.

1 Can Rita really count to ten?
2 Which of the principles of counting has Rita still to grasp?
3 Suggest some activities that might help to develop her counting skills.

DEVELOPING COUNTING

Plenty of everyday opportunities to practise and reinforce counting can be identified. Children enjoy counting, reciting numbers as they choose or distribute items, finding playmates for a game and so on. The one-to-one principle can be reinforced in many ways, matching brushes to paint pots, labels to milk bottles, buttons to buttonholes, knives to forks and so on. Ordinal numbers can also be introduced in a variety of practical ways – with model figures, with pictures and with activities – drawing attention to first, second, third and so on.

Number songs and rhymes and stories are always popular with pre-school children. Learning these songs and rhymes will make children familiar and confident with the order of counting words. 'One Man Went to Mow', and 'The Very Hungry Caterpillar' deal with numbers in ascending order while 'Ten In a Bed' and 'Five

Speckled Frogs' require counting down. The counting points are likely to be further emphasised if the songs are accompanied by some actions where the children can see the numbers building up or down.

GOOD PRACTICE

Pre-school staff must be aware of the complex nature of counting and provide for meaningful experiences and interactions that reinforce and develop children's skills.

As well as counting there are other aspects of number that children will develop in the pre-school years. They need to learn about conservation of number: that the number of items in a group stays the same however they are presented. Piaget held that children would not be able to conserve until they reached the concrete operations stage, that is at around seven years. However more recent research has challenged this, finding that children much younger than seven when presented with what seemed to be a more meaningful conservation task achieved success (Hughes, 1986). A child who can conserve number will recognise a group of, say, five model cars as five whether they are lined up bumper to bumper, piled on top of one another or stretched across the carpet. This 'fiveness' of five, the 'three-ness' of three and so on needs to be emphasised with children in their everyday activities.

A child who can conserve number will recognise that five is five, however it is presented

RECOGNISING NUMBERS

Numbers will be part of the child's environment in the same way that words and letters are. House numbers, car registration numbers, bus routes, price tickets, all of these, and many more, will contribute to an awareness of written numbers. Children are usually very keen to demonstrate their age with birthday badges cards and so on. Age numbers along with their own house number will be recognised by many quite young children. Birthdays can be marked in the childcare setting with cakes and candles and celebratory claps – one for every year – making a point of displaying the birthday number prominently. Pre-school centres often maintain a birthday poster where children find themselves named on the balloon or train carriage or cake that corresponds with the number for their age. This enables them to anticipate the move from one numbered division to the next. (**NB** Ensure that celebration of birthdays is acceptable for all children that you involve. Some religious groups may not approve of marking birthdays in this way.)

Children are usually keen to demonstrate their age with birthday badges and cards

Drawing attention to numbers in the environment can be a valuable activity in increasing children's familiarity with numbers and reinforces recognition. Look out for numbers on clothes, signs, clocks and so on.

Displaying a number line in the centre will help with recognition of numerals. A number line will also encourage children to practise the number sequence and assist them in 'counting on from' and 'counting back from'.

Using cards and posters and games that have been designed with number recognition in mind can be helpful. At this stage materials will be most effective if the one-to-one principle is emphasised by presenting the number symbol alongside the corresponding number of items, for example number games that help children to recognise the numeral by matching it with the same number of items.

GOOD PRACTICE

Include cultural diversity when investigating recognising and writing numbers. Display examples of different number systems alongside the children's attempts at devising their own ways of writing numbers. Some children may already be familiar with Punjabi, Urdu or Chinese numerals.

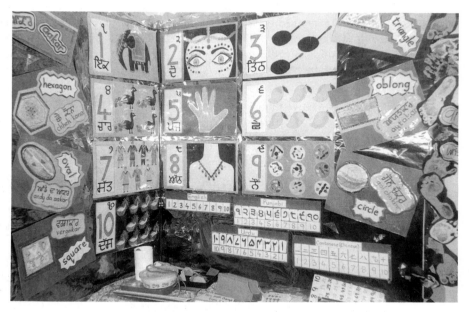

Show children that numerals can be written in many languages

WRITING NUMBERS

Children may find it difficult to understand the relationship between written numbers and real objects. Children experimenting with their own ways of writing numbers will often draw a picture or make a mark to represent each item (Hughes, 1986). This kind of representation reflects the one-to-one principle of counting and may appear more logical, with a mark for every item, than the system of numerals they will eventually learn. Learning to write numbers accurately is a challenging task for pre-school children and much practice will be required. Opportunities to practise writing numerals need to be provided at the pre-school stage but accurate writing should not be over-emphasised before giving children an opportunity to explore and understand the principle of representation of quantities. Getting children to use tallies to record counting can be a helpful stage in assisting understanding of this concept.

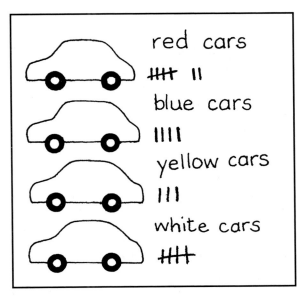

Children recorded cars passing by the nursery using a tally chart

NUMBER OPERATIONS

Pre-school children will be able to manage simple number operations of addition, subtraction, multiplication and division when these are linked to concrete objects in meaningful situations. These will occur as part of the children's play at activities in the nursery, such as adding together the wheels needed to construct a truck or the windows required for a Lego house. The organisation of the nursery can also provide opportunities to add and subtract. If the home corner can accommodate five children and there are three playing, then the children will know that two more can join them, thus demonstrating the calculation that three plus two equals five.

Subtraction can be demonstrated in similar ways with adults posing questions that encourage children to make a calculation and say what is left.

Sharing items between members of the group, whether it be the cars on the playmat or biscuits at snack time, will give children a practical experience of division. Cutting up apples, cake and sandwiches will also introduce discussion of fractional parts. The notion of 'fair shares' will appeal to children and underline the equal parts principle of division.

Multiplication can be demonstrated practically through activities such as looking at construction tasks – seeing that each car needs four wheels, and deciding how many wheels are needed for three cars, or deciding how many sweets will be needed to give two to each of four children. Posing and answering questions like these will help children towards understanding the link between multiplication and repeated addition.

Baking rock cakes

Darren was making rock cakes in the cooking area. He had mixed the ingredients together and was dividing the mixture into the cake tin. There were twelve sections in the pan and he had already filled five of them.

Nursery nurse: How many cakes are you going to make?
Darren: (touching each space) Twelve.
N.N: Have you made some already?
Darren: Yes, five.
N.N: How many more do you have to make?
Darren: (counts empty spaces) Seven.

He continued filling the spaces until the mixture was all gone. He noticed that some of the spaces contained lots of mixture while others contained very little.

Darren: No-one will want those little ones.

He then set about moving some mixture from the full to the less full tins.

1 What mathematical principles has Darren demonstrated?
2 What is the adult's role here?
3 How could Darren's learning be extended?

Opportunities for counting, comparison and calculation occur naturally in many activities

PROGRESS CHECK

1 What does counting involve?
2 How can you develop children's recognition of numbers?
3 How can you develop children's understanding of written numbers?

4 How can children of pre-school age develop an understanding of addition and subtraction? Give some examples.

Understanding and developing other areas of pre-school maths

As emphasised earlier in this chapter, pre-school maths is much broader than counting and number. This section will examine other elements of maths and suggest practical ways of providing for them within the framework of the activities that would usually be offered to children in the pre-school setting. For the children's mathematical understanding to be maximised, it is up to the pre-school worker to be aware of the potential for maths in any activity and to relate this to the individual child's capacity to understand. Skilful and sensitive structuring and intervention on the adult's part will encourage competence and confidence.

MEASURING

In the pre-school period children will begin to develop their experience and understanding of measuring, applying this to length and area, to volume and capacity, to weight, to time and to money. This will require familiarity with the language associated with measurement such as 'length', 'weight', etc. and comparative terms such as heavier, shorter and so on. Children will also be introduced to the practice of measuring with standard units – kilograms, minutes, centimetres, etc. – and non-standard units, which can be anything it seems appropriate to use, such as conkers to weigh against a book, or strides to measure the play area. As they become more familiar with the measuring process they can be encouraged to estimate before they measure and then compare their findings with the estimate.

Length and area
- Encourage children to compare their sizes. This would involve talking about tallest and shortest and perhaps presenting themselves in order, tallest to shortest, shortest to tallest.
- Make a height chart and measure with non-standard units say, handspans or Lego bricks.
- Measure everyday objects. Allow children to experiment using various units of measurement. They soon discover what works and what does not!
- Introduce standard measures by getting children used to handling centimetre tapes, rulers and trundle wheels. Talk about what things each measure is likely to be used for.
- Drawing around hands, feet or even whole bodies gives the children a chance to compare area.
- Covering tables and boxes with paper will give experience of area, that is measuring length and width at the same time. They can be encouraged to estimate, for example how many sheets of paper are needed.

Encourage children to compare heights and use mathematical language accurately

CASE STUDY

Measuring the playground

The children in the nursery had been talking about measuring and had been encouraged to join in a number of different measuring activities. They had used handspans, strides, pencils, Lego bricks and conkers. A group of older children decided that they wanted to measure the playground. After some discussion they settled on using pencils and began measuring, placing pencils end to end. The task proved too much for the children and they soon lost interest and gave up. At group time later that morning they talked about their difficulties and the nursery nurse suggested other ways of going about the task.

1 Why did this prove such a difficult task for the children?
2 What would you suggest to help them?
3 What did the children learn from this unsuccessful attempt?

Weight

- Give children plenty of practical experiences of holding things and talking about heavy and light, then comparing 'heavier than' and 'lighter than'. Encourage children to predict before holding.
- Use non-standard measures such as cups and spoons in cookery sessions as well as standard measures (though not in the same recipe!)
- Collect empty boxes and packets and find where and how the weight is written.
- Use balance scales and encourage children to select units to balance against. Shells, conkers or Lego could all be suitable. (Balance scales should be used as they demonstrate visually the equivalence principle of weighing.)
- Encourage discussions about size and weight. A house brick and a bag of sugar may be the same size but are they the same weight?
- Look at different types of scales and discuss what you would weigh on them. Children could weigh themselves using bathroom scales.

Volume and capacity

Volume is the amount of space taken up by an object. Capacity is the amount the object can contain.

- Introduce language associated with capacity such as 'full', 'half-full' and 'empty' (see case studies on pages 133 and 140).
- Give children plenty of opportunities to fill and empty containers of various shapes and sizes in the sand and water areas.
- Encourage the children to fill large containers with smaller ones.
- Get the children to estimate which container holds the most (or the least) and help devise a way to test this.

Give children plenty of opportunities to fill and empty containers of various shapes and sizes

- Collect bottles and packets and find how the capacity is recorded. Milk cartons and squash bottles will indicate millilitres or litres.
- Identify volume and capacity in other areas of play, for example: 'How many teacups will the teapot fill?' 'Will those bricks fit into that box?' 'How many beakers can be filled from that bottle of squash?'
- Draw attention to changes in volume, for example the cake that expands in the oven or the macaroni that swells in the pan.

Time
- The concept of measuring time is a very difficult one for pre-school children. Emphasising the daily routine shows children how the day is broken into sections.
- A pictorial chart of the daily routine can help children align themselves with where they are in the day. Children will respond to markers such as snack time, story time and home time.
- Choose stories and rhymes that deal with the passing of time such as 'Sleeping Beauty' and 'We're All Going To The Zoo Tomorrow'.
- Use group time to talk about past and future events and mark special events especially birthdays and annual festivals. This will emphasise the cycle of time.
- Introduce the calendar by talking about the day, for example, 'If it's Wednesday, we have music'.
- Waiting for cakes to bake gives children experience of the passing of a measured amount of time. Some children will use their own unit for measuring time, for example, 'It takes as long as Playbus'.
- Refer to clocks and watches and provide examples of different types, digital and analogue. Adding old wristwatches to the home corner may encourage children to incorporate time in their role play.

Money
- Use money in real situations such as nursery shopping for special activities (see the case study on page 131), collecting snack money or spending pocket money.
- Provide role play areas that involve the children in using money such as shops and cafés. Use price lists and tickets so that children try to match the coins with the price.
- Provide plenty of opportunities for children to handle money, real or play, getting them to sort the coins into different denominations. Children who have pocket money quickly learn about the equivalence of coins, accepting two 5p pieces for one 10p.

PATTERN

Pattern occurs both in number and shape. It is an important mathematical concept that lays the foundation for algebra. The essential features of pattern are that it is regular and predictable, and children need to be alerted to these characteristics. The following will help children to achieve an understanding of pattern.
- Identifying pattern by looking for it in the environment. Pattern can be found in

brick walls, on floor tiles, on curtains and carpets and on clothes. Pattern can also be identified in nature in animal markings, in seed heads, in plants and so on.

- Providing plenty of opportunities for children to create their own patterns. This can be done in painting, printing and collage activities. Children can make 3D patterns with beads, bricks and natural materials. They can print patterns on their own fabric and wrapping paper. Children may need adult assistance to help them identify and keep to their pattern.
- Encouraging children to copy and continue patterns. This can be in 2D – with drawing, painting and collage – but more often in 3D with bricks, beads, on peg boards and so on. Computer programmes on pattern are readily available, too.

SHAPE

Children need to be able to recognise and understand the properties of common two- and three- dimensional shapes.

- Encourage children to identify shapes in the environment, recognising wheels as circles, doors as rectangles or the post box as a cylinder.
- Introduce children to recognising and naming shapes. It is important to use the correct terms. Include circle, square, rectangle, triangle and oval. Some three-dimensional shapes may be less familiar but include cube, cuboid, sphere, cylinder, cone, prism, pyramid and ovoid. Sets of geometric shapes are available to demonstrate the more unusual figures and children may find it helpful if the unfamiliar term is associated with a familiar object such as linking 'ovoid' with an egg.

Children will begin to understand the properties of shapes if they handle the shapes frequently

- Children will only become conversant with the properties of shapes if they have plenty of opportunities to handle them. Point out curves, faces and vertices to them. Get them to draw around shapes and to print with the faces of 3D shapes. Compare 2D and 3D shapes.
- Building bricks and other construction equipment can give children firsthand experience of the properties of different shapes.
- Sorting boxes for box modelling – building models from empty boxes, usually packaging, and other scrap materials – can help children distinguish between shapes and reinforce knowledge of their properties.
- Use different shapes of paper for collage, drawing and painting.
- Children can cut and roll their own shapes with clay and playdough.
- Encouraging children to fit shapes together in patterns will enable them to discover which shapes tessellate.

SETS AND SORTING

Sorting and classifying objects into sets contributes to the development of logical thinking. It requires recognition of the feature that characterises the set, for example they are all red or all round or all animals. Pre-school children may find it difficult to sort for more than one characteristic (or attribute) at a time. Presented with a box of plastic figures, a three-year-old would be able to sort all the green figures and then all the cars. Sorting for all green cars would be a much more difficult task. Sorting and classifying skills can be developed through the following activities.

- Provide boxes and trays containing collections of shells, beads, buttons, etc. and encourage children to devise their own criteria for sorting.
- Use special sorting equipment and encourage children to sort for particular attributes. Introduce appropriate language where necessary.
- Encourage children to verbalise their reasons for including or excluding certain items when sorting. You may be surprised by their reasoning.
- Provide opportunities for recording sets. Hoops or circles are useful as are special trays. Older children may record their findings pictorially.
- Encourage sorting and classifying through everyday activities. Clearing up, tidying away and sorting materials for craft sessions will provide these opportunities.

CASE STUDY

Sorting animals
The nursery children had been working around the theme of animals for some weeks. This had included all kinds of activities that involved animals as well as discussions about pets, a visit to a farm and animal stories songs and rhymes. A group of children were sitting with a nursery nurse at the sorting trays. A large number of brightly coloured plastic animal shapes was available and the children were being encouraged first to identify them and then decide on how to sort them. They began with the most obvious attribute of colour and then went on to make sets of pets, farm

animals and animals that can fly. When they came to making a set of animals that ate grass the nursery nurse became aware of a heated discussion. One child was insisting that alongside the cows, sheep, horses and goats they should include cats. When questioned as to whether he was really sure about cats eating grass he said that his own cat did eat grass whenever it was in the garden and that cats should be included in the set. The cat was allowed to stay, despite some misgivings on the part of the others in the group.

1 What does this tell you about this child's ability to sort?
2 What are the implications for the adult's role here?

PROGRESS CHECK

1 What general principles should be followed when providing for pre-school maths?
2 What do children need to know about measuring?
3 Suggest some ways of developing children's understanding of pattern.
4 How is sorting linked to the development of logical thinking?

Promoting pre-school maths

As with any other area of the curriculum, the adult's role is crucial both in the provision of an environment rich in potential for mathematics and through their sensitive and knowledgeable interaction with children within that environment. The pre-school worker can support the development of mathematical understanding in the following ways.

■ Being aware of the mathematical potential of activities provided in the nursery.
■ Including mathematical objectives in planning.
■ Approaching maths with a positive and confident attitude. Remember that your attitude will influence the children's own attitudes towards maths.
■ Introducing mathematical terminology accurately and in the appropriate context.
■ Devising problem-solving situations where children can apply their mathematical knowledge.
■ Observing progress on an individual level and planning for that child's next step.
■ Making links between children's experiences at home with those at nursery, promoting awareness of the maths in everyday activities.
■ Questioning and commenting in ways that help children consolidate their knowledge and move forward in their understanding.
■ Enabling children to record their mathematical findings in ways that are meaningful and appropriate.

Adults can help children record their work in ways that are appropriate

KEY TERMS

You need to know what these words and phrases mean. Go back through the chapter and make sure that you understand:

capacity
cardinal numbers
computation
conservation of number
consolidate understanding
logical thinking
number operations
one-to-one principle

ordinal numbers
sorting and classifying skills
standard measures / non-standard
    measures
superlatives
tallies
volume

Further reading

Hughes, M., *Children and Number*, Blackwell, 1986
Richards, R. and Jones, L., *An Early Start to Mathematics*, Simon & Schuster, 1990

8 KNOWLEDGE AND UNDERSTANDING OF THE WORLD

> **This chapter covers:**
> - Early geographical concepts
> - Early historical concepts
> - Introducing science
> - Introducing technology
> - Further reading

The area of learning of the Knowledge and Understanding of the World in the pre-school curriculum provides a foundation for historical, geographical, scientific and technological learning. The aim is to develop children's awareness of the world around them, their environment, people and features of the natural and man-made world. Noticing similarities and differences, patterns and change are an important part of this emerging knowledge.

> *Children talk about where they live, their environment, their families past and present and events in their lives. They explore and recognise features of living things, objects and events in the natural and man-made world and look closely at similarities, differences, patterns and change. They show an awareness of the purposes of some features of the area in which they live. They talk about their observations, sometimes recording them and ask questions to gain information about why things happen and how things work. They explore and select materials and equipment and use skills such as cutting, joining, folding and building for a variety of purposes. They use technology, where appropriate to support learning.*
> (Desirable Outcomes for Children's Learning, *DfEE with SCAA, 1996*)

Early geographical concepts

Geography, at this stage of development, is concerned with an awareness of the environment and the significance of features within it. The starting point for this needs to be the immediate, familiar environment of home and school. Children need to develop an awareness of both natural and man-made features in the environment.

THE LOCAL ENVIRONMENT

This may include an awareness of:
- buildings and their usage
- open spaces, their features and usage
- the use of space and size

- the pattern of seasons
- weather and its importance
- relevant geographical features such as hills, rivers, woods, sea, and so on
- symbols used, for example road signs and road markings,

GOOD PRACTICE

As children learn through direct experience with the world much of this learning can be achieved through going out into the local environment. This may be to observe certain features, such as buildings or to experience certain conditions such as wind or rain. There needs to be a focus to what the children are observing and/or experiencing and an adult to draw their attention to relevant features in the environment.

The active experience of going out into the local environment can be followed up in a number of ways:
- by individual and group discussion
- through role play and imaginary play
- by recording through painting and drawing
- by modelling, with a variety of materials.

CASE STUDY

Developing an awareness of natural and man-made features in the environment (1)

A group of children, accompanied by an adult, went for a walk in the local area. The children had been asked to look at the buildings and identify the different types of homes that people had. On the walk the adult drew the children's attention to flats, houses and bungalows. They looked at the homes and discussed their features. The children talked about their own homes and identified the type of home they had.

At grouptime the children reported back to all the others what they saw and identified the different types of homes in pictures that the adult had provided. They discussed the similarities and differences between the different types of homes.

Later in the day the children were encouraged to represent something that they had seen, either by painting or drawing or through modelling. The adult discussed with the children the activities that they were involved in, encouraging the children to name the type of home and its features. The work was displayed as part of the work on 'Where we live'.

1 How did the adult ensure that the activity was at the children's level?
2 What new and/or different concepts could the children develop through this activity?
3 How could the adult extend this learning in other activities?
4 What was the value of displaying the children's work in this instance?

Early geographical skills include an awareness of the environment and the significance of the features within it

CASE STUDY

Developing an awareness of natural and man-made features in the environment (2)

On a rainy day a child who was looking out of the nursery window asked, 'What is rain?' An adult took the child outside and they let the rain fall on their hands and faces. They felt that it was wet and talked about where it was coming from. Back inside the adult and the child looked at a book about water together. They discussed all the different ways in which we use water.

Later the same day in the home corner the adult observed the child 'bathing the baby' and then giving her a drink.

1 How did the adult develop the child's interest?
2 Why is this important?
3 How did the adult make the learning relevant to the child?
4 How was this child able to consolidate his learning?
5 What early geographical concepts was the child able to explore?

Displaying children's work encourages the children's interest

Children's play provides opportunities for them to develop and explore their understanding of the world

SPATIAL RELATIONSHIPS

The language of spatial relationships is an important aspect of the geography and maths curriculum. Children need a wide variety of experience to develop these concepts.

At this level this includes concepts such as:

- bigger than and smaller than
- under and over
- next to
- behind and in front
- right and left.

GOOD PRACTICE

These concepts must be developed in a concrete way. Children need to be able to clearly see the spatial relationship between two items. Good practice requires the context of this learning to be realistic and relevant to the child, for example an adult may comment that a child is sitting 'next to me' or comment that a child is 'sitting in front of me' at a group storytime. These opportunities arise throughout the day and, where and when appropriate these concepts can be introduced. Activities that develop these concepts can also be planned, for example, play with large bricks where the adult focuses the activity on building towers and, with the children, compares them as bigger than or smaller than each other.

CASE STUDY

Developing concepts of spatial relationships

A four-year-old was playing on the car mat. She was driving the cars around the town, shopping, going to the library, going swimming and going to the park. An adult observed the child for a short time before joining in the play and driving a car around the mat. In discussing where each of them was going and how they were going to get there the adult introduced the concepts of behind, in front, left, right, under and over. The concepts were introduced at the appropriate time when the cars were in the appropriate position.

1 Why was it important that the adult observed the child's play before joining in?
2 Why was this a good opportunity to introduce these concepts?
3 During this play sequence how could the adult check which concepts the child has already acquired?

DISTANCE AND DIRECTION

Distance and direction are important geographical concepts. Both these concepts are difficult for young children to grasp as they require an understanding of time and place, which are abstract concepts. Early experiences, therefore, need to be

A concept of spatial relationships needs to be developed in a meaningful way.

clearly referenced to their own experiences of distance and direction. This may include:

- talking about the journey from home to nursery
- talking about familiar journeys to shops, grandparents' house and friends
- discussion of the mode of transport used and why
- discussion of why people travel to different places, for example to work, to go on holiday and to buy things
- stories and activities that involve a journey.

GOOD PRACTICE

These are difficult concepts for young children to grasp and, therefore, at this stage of development, they will talk about journeys in the broadest terms, for example 'It's a long way' or 'It's not far'. Children need to be encouraged to recognise similarities and differences in how and why we travel.

CASE STUDY

Going on a journey

The children's story 'A Bear Hunt' by Michael Rosen was read to a group of children. The children discussed the journey to look for the bear, sequencing the events both there and back. The adult extended this story session by getting the children to act out the bear hunt.

Some children noticed that coming back from the bear hunt was the same as the journey there. They returned to the book and, in discussion, noticed that the journey was the opposite way round on the way back. This led to discussion about their journeys to the nursery and what they saw on the journey at the beginning and at the end depending on whether they were coming to nursery or going home.

1 Why is this an appropriate way to introduce the concepts of distance and direction to young children?
2 How could the drama session help the children to understand distance and direction?
3 What important concept about direction had the children noticed from this book?
4 Why is it important to relate this concept to the children's everyday lives?

PROGRESS CHECK

1 Outline the type of experiences necessary for children of this age to develop an awareness of the environment.
2 List the natural and man-made features that young children need to become aware of.
3 What are spatial relationships?
4 How would you begin to develop an awareness of spatial relationships in young children?
5 Why are distance and direction difficult concepts for young children to grasp?
6 What would be your approach to developing these concepts in young children?

Early historical concepts

At pre-school level a sense of history is concerned with an understanding of the different ways in which people live, and lived, and with the concept of the passage of time. These are very difficult concepts for young children. They require an understanding of the abstract concepts of time and space.

Young children tend to live in the here and now. The passage of time is marked by events such as meal times, bathtime, visits in the near future or recent past. Sequences of events such as the pattern of the pre-school session also mark out time for young children. They do not divide time into standard units of minutes, hours, days and dates.

A sense of history is also concerned with an understanding of the different ways in which people lived through time. It is important to realise that young children are not yet able to clearly differentiate between fantasy and reality, therefore what may be a historical fact to adults may appear unreal and story-like to a young child.

GOOD PRACTICE

Young children need direct experience in a concrete way to enable them to assimilate and accommodate information. Ways, therefore, need to be found to introduce ideas of how people lived in the past and live now in a way that is appropriate and accessible to young children. The aim is to engage children's imagination and feeling for a particular time or event.

Edwards (1994) develops the idea of 'leftovers' a good way of introducing the idea of how people used to live. Leftovers are everyday items from the past that children can compare with their own experiences of living today. This allows children direct experience with articles on which to build their concepts. Children need to handle and use these articles, where appropriate, to get a real feeling for what used to be.

The passage of time also needs to be linked to concrete situations. The routine of a day or a session at pre-school provides valuable markers of time for young children. The routine needs to be made explicit to the children and discussed in terms of what comes next. Other daily routines can be discussed in terms of their place in the pattern of a day, for example getting up and bathtime.

Birthdays, growing up and getting older are relevant experiences of time for young children. These need to be shown in clear, concrete terms, for example a year time line with all the children's birthdays on it, photographs of the staff and/or children as babies, a ritual to celebrate children's birthdays and getting grandparents or older people to come and talk to the children about their own childhood.

Personal and family histories introduce ideas of how people lived in the past and how they live now, in a way that is accessible to children

CASE STUDY

Developing a concept of time (1)

A playgroup assistant was washing the painting aprons in a bowl of soapy water, helped by a group of children. A child commented that they did not wash clothes like that at home, that they used a washing machine. The adult discussed with the children how and why clothes were washed.

The adult continued this theme at storytime with the book *Doing the Washing* by Sarah Garland.

The adult began the following session with the same story. The group again talked about the way in which their clothes were washed and the adult introduced a washboard and a dolly peg and tub to the children and showed them how people used to wash their clothes. They were then put in the home corner for the children to play with.

In this way the children were able to have direct and relevant experience with the past. The adult had engaged the children's interest and imagination in developing a feeling of past and present that enabled them to compare the past and the present in a way that was meaningful to them.

1 How did the adult make this experience relevant to the children?
2 What is significant about her starting point?
3 List other examples of ways in which the past can be made relevant to young children.

'Leftovers' are a good way for young children to begin to develop a concept of the past

Developing a concept of time (2)

At group time an adult showed the children four photographs of a baby, a child, a teenager and an adult. They discussed the photographs in terms of which was a baby etc. and how they knew this. The children commented on the size of the people and tried to guess how old they were.

Eventually the adult told the children that all the pictures were of the same person and asked them how could that be possible because they were all different. They discussed their own families and the idea of growing up.

The adult asked the children if they could bring in a photograph of themselves as a baby and she put up a notice requesting the same. As children brought in their photographs they were put on a pinboard titled 'Guess who I am'. The children enjoyed looking at the photographs and guessing.

Some time later the adult went through the pictures with the group and identified the children. They discussed how they had guessed who was who. The children were able to recognise that there were similarities between the babies and the children's features and that the babies had grown up.

1 How does this experience help a child to develop a concept of time?
2 Why is this an appropriate way to begin to develop a concept of time?
3 Think of other ways in which this concept could be introduced to young children.

PROGRESS CHECK

1 What early historical concepts are appropriate to pre-school children?
2 Why are these difficult concepts for young children to acquire?
3 Describe good practice in introducing these concepts to young children.
4 Give some examples of good practice.
5 Identify some other ways in which these concepts can be introduced to young children.

Introducing science

Science at pre-school level is concerned with fundamental concepts and skills. Skills that are appropriate at pre-school level include sorting, classifying and comparing and methods of enquiry such as asking questions, investigating and observing. From these activities conceptual awareness can be developed.

Using personal experience helps children develop a concept of time

SORTING, CLASSIFYING AND COMPARING

These are important early science skills. There are many opportunities within a pre-school setting where children sort and classify items, for example when tidying up or selecting a particular toy to pack into a box. This skill can be extended through sorting and classifying games and activities where the child's attention is drawn to the fact that they are selecting and classifying according to specific criteria, for example red ones, wooden ones, dolls' clothes, balls and blocks. Initially, children will be able to sort according to only one criteria. Once this skill is established two criteria may be introduced, for example red cars or metal spoons.

ASKING QUESTIONS

Children need to be encouraged to ask how and why questions, to be inquisitive and curious. These skills are fundamental to science at all levels. Initially the questions may come from the adult, encouraging the children to seek explanations. The way in which the questions are asked is essential to good practice. The questions need to be open ended and the response positive and encouraging. This is important as children's responses may not always be accurate because of their limited conceptual development. Questions can also be used to develop children's concepts. The adult needs to structure her questions to focus the child's attention in a particular direction or to encourage a child to try and predict what might happen.

Sorting, classifying and comparing are important early science skills

INVESTIGATING

Investigating at pre-school level will be as a result of interaction with the environment through a child's five senses. These firsthand experiences enable children to develop an understanding of the properties of materials and how and why things happen. Sensitive questioning can focus the child's attention on significant points.

Children need the opportunity to investigate a wide range of materials and living things. They need to be encouraged to use all their senses when investigating.

OBSERVATION

Observation is an important skill. Children need to be encouraged to develop careful and focused observation skills. This can be achieved across a wide range of pre-school activities. Children learn through different senses and in different ways and, therefore, it is important that there is the opportunity for the information to be acquired in a multi-sensory way. This must be considered when planning to ensure that all children's needs are met. The important factor is that children are encouraged to observe closely and carefully and, where appropriate, to describe details of what they have seen. Magnifying glasses, binoculars and microscopes can be introduced where and when appropriate. It is important to note that some children may not be able to associate these items with their enlargement properties.

As with all learning at pre-school level children need firsthand, concrete experiences to make their learning meaningful. The pattern outlined by Moyles (see page 36) of free and guided play experiences is particularly important with science-based activities. Young children need an adult to interpret and guide their learning. The adult's role is not one of directive teaching but a drawing out of the necessary concepts and skills. This requires the adult to have a sensitive awareness of the child's level of understanding and of the ways in which children acquire concepts.

CASE STUDY

Making a rain hat for teddy

Children were supplied with a variety of different materials, a water squirter and paper. The playworker discussed what we wear in the rain and why. The group identified the fact that the hat they were going to make must be water resistant.

The children were then asked how they thought they could find out which of the materials was the best for making teddy's hat. They observed the equipment and discussed what they were going to do.

The children decided that the material that they needed should not let the water go through it. After much discussion they decided that the way to achieve this would be to put a piece of each material onto a piece of paper and squirt water onto it then look at the paper to see if it was wet. If the water had gone through the material and wet the paper it would not be good material for a hat. The children did this and found an appropriate material and made the hat. They then tested their results by taking the teddy outside in the rain!

This activity enabled the children to develop a range of methods of enquiry and concepts. They ware able to ask and answer questions, predict outcomes, then investigate this in a concrete and meaningful way. They then observed, discussed and tested the outcomes. The adult was a vital part of this activity. Her role was to carefully guide the children's learning through careful questioning and answering. In this way she could direct the children's attention towards relevant concepts and encourage development of the necessary skills.

1 Why was this a meaningful activity for young children?
2 What concepts could be developed in this activity?
3 What methods of enquiry did the children use and/or develop?
4 Why was the adult's role vital in this activity?

PROGRESS CHECK

1 What methods of enquiry are appropriate for young children to develop?
2 How can conceptual awareness be developed?
3 Why is it important to encourage children to ask questions?

4 What is the adult's role in asking and answering questions?
5 Describe how children develop investigative skills.
6 Outline some opportunities across the curriculum for young children to develop observation skills.
7 Why is a combination of free and guided play important in developing early science skills?

Introducing technology

Technology at pre-school level involves early designing and making skills at a basic level of cutting, joining and building things in different ways. Children need to be encouraged to try different ways of achieving their aim. The early scientific skills of questioning, investigating and observation are important to successful design and construction.

Alongside their own experimental learning the use and importance of technology in our everyday lives need to be drawn to children's attention. This can be achieved through informal observation and discussion of the use of every day equipment such as telephones and computers. Artefacts can also be brought into the nursery to enable the children to have firsthand experience of operating and investigating technology, for example old clocks for the children to observe and investigate cogs, wheels and hinges.

Technology can also be used to support children's learning across the curriculum, for example computers, television, video recorders and electronic keyboards.

GOOD PRACTICE

Children need the time, space and relevant materials to experiment and investigate different ways of cutting, joining and building. This free play and experimentation is essential for developing the initial skills involved in the construction of items. Consolidation of these initial skills, through free play is necessary at all stages of development.

As children progress and develop these initial skills they can be encouraged to refine their constructed items through trial, observation and experimentation. The aim of this is to enable children to consider the design of an item appropriate to its usage. These are complex skills and staff must be aware of the needs and abilities of each individual child when planning these activities. Scaffolding children's play in this way (see Bruner, page 34) must be done in a sensitive way, no child must be made to feel that their item is substandard and must be improved.

In a child's investigation of existing technology a supportive adult is necessary to ask questions and focus the child's attention on relevant details. As with science skills the adult's method of questioning is essential to developing the child's concepts of how things work and the reason for their usage.

A child demonstrates early designing and making skills

Making a Grand Prix car

Amelia, a four-year-old had seen the Grand Prix on television at the week-end. On Monday morning she got the car track out and set it up. Unfortunately she could only find motor cars to use on the track and not Formula One cars. The nursery nurse suggested that she make one as they did not have any.

First, they looked in detail at one of the nursery cars. They then discussed what are the similarities and differences between this and a Formula One car. They considered the design of the car and the materials that they would need. They collected the materials and the nursery nurse encouraged Amelia to plan how she would make the car. Together they built the car, discussing the size, the shape, how to join the pieces and fix on the wheels. Amelia made the decisions including deciding that sticky tape was the best way to join all the parts together and fix on the wheels.

Having built the car Amelia went to play with it on the car track. The nursery nurse joined her in the play later. While they were playing together Amelia commented that the wheels did not go around like those on real cars and the toy cars in the nursery, and that it would be more fun if they would. Together they returned to the collage table and looked at all the different type of fasteners available. They experimented with the fasteners by joining two pieces of card together to see if they created a wheel action. Eventually they decided to use a split pin to join Amelia's wheels to her car. The wheels now went around as she pushed the car on the track.

In this activity Amelia was able to use early technology skills to enrich her imaginative play. She was able to identify a need for technology. She made an initial plan and implemented her idea taking account of size, shape and materials. As she used her car she was able to identify a difficulty with the initial design and, with guidance, improve her design. The activity was also a good example of building on a child's own interests to develop concepts and skills.

1 What aspects of technology were evident in this activity?
2 How was design and making an item made relevant to Amelia?
3 How did the adult support Amelia's learning?

PROGRESS CHECK

1 Describe early technology for young children.
2 What are the ways in which early technology skills can be achieved?
3 What links are there with early science skills?

KEY TERMS

You need to know what these words and phrases mean. Go back through the chapter and make sure that you understand:

abstract concepts	natural world
concrete learning	spatial relationships
man-made world	standard units of time

Further reading

Edwards, A. and Knight, P., *Effective Early Years Education*, Open University Press, 1994
Matusiak, C., *Foundations for the Early Years*, Scholastic Publications Ltd, 1992

9 *PHYSICAL DEVELOPMENT*

> **This chapter covers:**
> - **Understanding physical development**
> - **Providing for the development of fine motor skills**
> - **Providing for the development of gross motor skills**
> - **The adult's role in promoting physical development**

During their pre-school years children need to be given opportunities in both indoor and outdoor environments to develop a range of physical skills. These will include manipulative skills as well as skills associated with mobility and control of the body. These early experiences will have a part to play in establishing a positive attitude to exercise and an active way of life.

> *Children move confidently and imaginatively with increasing control and co-ordination and an awareness of space and others. They use a range of small and large equipment and balancing and climbing apparatus, with increasing skill. They handle appropriate tools, objects, construction and malleable materials safely and with increasing control.*
> (Desirable Outcomes for Children's Learning, *DfEE with SCAA, 1996*)

Understanding physical development

Physical development is concerned with the growth, development and control of the movement of the body. It comprises:
- fine motor skills – manipulative skills, hand-eye co-ordination
- gross motor skills – whole body and limb movements, balance, whole body co-ordination

Children develop these skills through a process of practice and refinement. They need to be provided with opportunities for this through a range of activities within the pre-school setting. As with all other areas of development, within any group of children of a similar age there will be a wide variation in terms of capability. This must be borne in mind when planning, and provision should be made for the full spectrum of abilities. Children will be able to develop new skills only when they are physiologically and psychologically ready. Adults need to watch for this readiness by observing the children in their play and then provide a framework for them to practise and refine these skills. Within this framework, adults can 'scaffold' children's learning by intervening in the play and assisting at a level that is appropriate to the child, enabling the skill to be developed. Careful observation of the child will indicate the competence already achieved and thus the skills that might be within the child's grasp when given assistance.

PROGRESS CHECK

1 What is physical development?
2 Why is readiness an important aspect of children's physical development?
3 How can we provide for children's physical development?

Providing for the development of fine motor skills

Opportunities for children to develop their fine motor skills exist in everyday routine tasks as much as in the activities provided as part of a pre-school programme. Worthwhile activities provide for a number of areas of development simultaneously, rather than for one in isolation. However, it is helpful to identify how certain activities contribute to the development of fine motor skills, as well as to consider the range of abilities that can be provided for within each area.

GOOD PRACTICE

Children need to be presented with activities that are within the range of their capabilities and that are challenging but not frustrating. Practice is the key to achieving competence and it is, therefore, important that children have adequate opportunity to repeat activities many times. Staff need to encourage children by acknowledging progress and offering help when appropriate.

This section gives some examples of activities that require fine motor skills.
- Self-care routines practise skills such as buttoning clothes, fastening zips and tying laces. Using a knife and fork will require some perseverance. Competence in these self-care skills is closely linked to self esteem, and thought should be given to choosing clothes for children so that they can manage to dress themselves independently.
- Malleable materials such as playdough, clay and Plasticine will provide children with a chance to pinch, roll, knead and twist. When tools are used, cutting, pushing and pressing will be practised. Using a variety of materials will present a challenge as some are more resistant than others.
- Puzzles and games can provide for a range of abilities. Jigsaw pieces that are large and thick will be easier to pick up and position than small, thin pieces. A range of different levels should be provided. Games that require the moving of pieces around a board develop hand-eye co-ordination. Threading and peg-board type activities will develop hand-eye co-ordination along with manipulative skills.
- The home corner or dramatic play area will contain items to open and close. Dolls may be dressed and undressed, 'tea' poured and dressing-up clothes fastened.
- Painting and creative activities require hand-eye co-ordination and manipulative skills. The size of paper supplied and the type of brushes should reflect the capability of the child. Collage activities that need cutting, positioning and glueing can

Getting dressed requires children to use their manipulative skills

be very demanding. Some children may be able to manage simple sewing. Using scissors can be a difficult skill to refine.

- Small construction apparatus of various types should be available. Some will be more difficult to manipulate than others and pre-school staff should check that there is suitable provision for all children. Familiarity with the equipment will develop confidence and lead to its use in more complex ways. Children need plenty of time to experiment with the fitting and fixing process that this equipment demands before they can realise the full potential of the activity.
- Holding a book, turning the pages and following the sequence of pictures or text requires hand-eye co-ordination and manipulative skills. Finger rhymes also practise manipulative skills.
- Most pre-school centres provide a writing table where children can practise with the tools of writing. Thick pencils or pencil grips will be helpful to some children. Different types of writing media will present problems of pressure and control to solve.
- Sand and water play will give children a chance to fill and empty containers practising hand-eye co-ordination. Fastening lids and unscrewing bottle caps will test manipulative skills. Picking up small items from sand or water provides another challenge.

Familiarity with equipment will enable children to use it in complex ways

- Using a computer keyboard requires precise manipulative control and hand-eye co-ordination. Given enough practice, children will acquire these skills and manage complex operations. Less experienced children may not be so confident but should be encouraged to persevere.
- A technology centre that encourages use of tools in woodwork or in assembling or taking apart will provide an interesting focus for practising fine motor skills.

CASE STUDY

Cutting and collage

Philip, aged three, was quite new to nursery and already showing lots of interest in any activity that involved sticking. He enjoyed making collage pictures and box-modelling. The nursery nurse noticed that he rarely used scissors, preferring to tear paper to the size and shape that he wanted. When some fabric was included for collage he was unable to tear it and struggled to cut it with scissors. The nursery nurse sat by him and showed him how to place his fingers in the scissors and she held the fabric as he cut it, explaining what she was doing. He made some progress with the cutting but still seemed uncomfortable. When he put down the scissors and started to spread the glue the nursery nurse noticed that he used his left hand more readily than his right. When left-handed scissors were given to him he was able to cut through the fabric easily and, with some help and encouragement, completed his picture in a short time.

1 Why did the nursery nurse intervene here?
2 How can you help children to use tools effectively?

GOOD PRACTICE

Children need good quality tools that are appropriate for their purpose. They will soon become frustrated if the scissors will not cut through paper or fabric, or the saw makes no impression on the wood. Adults should teach the safe and effective use of tools and supervise their use closely.

PROGRESS CHECK

1 Why is it important that children are given the opportunity to repeat activities?
2 Through what kinds of activities do children develop their fine motor skills?
3 Any group of children will have within it a range of physical capabilities. How can you provide for this?

Providing for the development of gross motor skills

As with fine motor skills, children will develop gross motor skills through a very wide range of activities and everyday experiences. The pre-school curriculum should provide opportunities for regular physical activity in both indoor and outdoor settings.

Children need physical activity to promote the healthy growth of bones, muscles, the heart and lungs. Exercise also aids digestion and is a factor in establishing patterns of rest and sleep. Vigorous physical play in early childhood may also help to establish positive attitudes to exercise that stay with the child into adult life.

When planning for physical play for children, the following general points should be taken into account.

■ Physical activities should be planned to meet the needs of the whole ability range. They should provide a challenge to every child at a level that is appropriate for the individual.

■ Safety must have a high priority. This will include checking equipment, providing safe surfaces, ensuring proper supervision and making sure that children understand the rules of playing safely.

■ Some children will be less confident in their physical abilities and will need time to watch before they join in. They need to feel that they can participate at their own pace. Very few children will be confident beyond their physical abilities, where they get themselves into situations that they cannot manage. However, this may occur and needs to be recognised.

■ Children need opportunities to practice the same skill, sometimes in the same context, many times before they become competent.

■ Physical activities will promote many areas of development. Sharing equipment or space and negotiating the rules of a game will require social skills. Setting and achieving individual targets contributes to the child's self esteem and emotional development. Planning and problem-solving in physical activities will provide an intellectual challenge.

THE IMPORTANCE OF OUTDOOR PLAY

Most pre-school centres will provide children with an opportunity for on-site, outdoor play on a regular, often daily, basis. Some may even be designed with the British climate in mind and include covered outdoor play space that can be used in poor weather conditions.

GOOD PRACTICE

As with other areas, children's outdoor play will be enhanced by adult involvement. Adults should observe children and identify opportunities to extend learning. This could be teaching and practising a new skill, for example throwing and catching a beanbag or it could be helping solve a problem with, say, a traffic layout or it could be organising a game. Staffing levels for outdoor play should provide for interaction as well as supervision.

Children's play will be enhanced by adult involvement

Outdoor play provides the following benefits.

- An opportunity to be out in the fresh air although, realistically, this would have to balanced against hazards of sunburn and air pollution.
- Space that will allow for vigorous movement such as running and climbing and access to large equipment. The chance to release energy in this way will usually be restricted in an indoor environment.
- The opportunity to make more noise than is acceptable indoors. Children will understand the need to maintain a quieter indoor environment if they have a chance to be noisy outdoors.
- A rich sensory experience where children can experience different materials – leaves, twigs, pebbles, stones – and can develop awareness of concepts such as wind, rain, temperature, light and shade.

PROVIDING FOR PHYSICAL PLAY

The following section looks at ways of providing for aspects of physical play and assumes that outside space is available for activities. When no outdoor play is possible, provision for gross motor development will need to be made as part of indoor planning.

It is not expected that all of these activities would be available at every session. Staff need to plan for physical play in the same way that they plan for other areas of the curriculum and provide a balanced programme. Physical play that is always presented to children in exactly the same way with the same layout and same equipment may fail to interest children and engage them in purposeful play. In this case, it will be necessary to make significant changes to re-activate interest. However, it should be remembered that children need to repeat and practise skills many times and that the physical play environment should provide for this continuity within a framework that remains inviting.

Physical play activities can be linked to themes followed across other areas of the curriculum. From time to time, provision might be directed to a physical theme, for example equipment and games that emphasise balance and direction.

Spatial awareness

Children need to learn about and control their bodies in relation to space, other people and objects. This concept of spatial awareness needs to be developed so that children can move safely and with confidence in their environment. Games that encourage moving backwards, forwards and sideways, turning, moving in front of, behind and next to will be helpful here. Many ring games are based around these kinds of actions. Ring games also encourage children to synchronise their movements with others. This vocabulary of direction and position needs to be frequently reinforced alongside actions. The game of Simon Says may be useful for this purpose, though with small groups and in short bursts with pre-school children.

Large apparatus

Large apparatus such as climbing frames, slides and balancing planks and benches will provide children with opportunities to climb, jump, crawl and balance.

Equipment should be chosen and set up with different heights and levels to provide a challenge to children of all abilities. If possible some provision should be made for gripping and hanging actions that promote upper body strength. Barrels, tunnels, crates and planks can be used in flexible ways and may be arranged according to children's plans. Including drapes and blankets to allow for the enclosure of spaces will stimulate imaginative play. Some large apparatus is very versatile and can be set up in a number of ways, indoors as well as outdoors. It may be possible to encourage particular kinds of movement, for example crawling, according to the combination you present.

Large apparatus should provide children with opportunities to stretch and grip

Small apparatus

Children need to begin to learn the skills of catching and throwing and ball control. At this age there will be substantial differences in children's physical co-ordination, balance and manual dexterity, all of which will affect these skills. Choose equipment carefully. Beanbags and quoits are easier to catch than balls. A football is too large and hard for small children who need to practise kicking and dribbling with a smaller, softer ball. Adults need to work with children to teach and practise these skills as children will find it difficult to throw accurately to one another and become frustrated. Competitive games are not appropriate at this stage because of the wide ability range, but children can be encouraged to compete against their own previous performance in simple games such as throwing a beanbag into a hoop.

Wheeled toys

These are very popular in most centres and will include tricycles, trucks, wheelbarrows, prams and trolleys among others. As with other equipment, care should be taken that the full ability range is catered for. Most children will be able to pedal a tricycle at three years of age but some may not yet have mastered the co-ordination necessary and will still be 'scooting'. Play on wheeled toys requires co-ordination, control and directional awareness. Slopes in the surface will allow children on wheeled toys to explore the scientific principle of forces at first hand. Road markings and traffic signals can be used to encourage more structured play.

Playground play

Children need space where they can run, jump, hop and skip and many will organise their own games and routines that involve these actions. Adults can encourage them by devising simple games that include moving in particular ways, for example a variation of the game of Pigeon Steps. Hard surfaces can be marked out with a number of designs that provoke interest and encourage children to experiment with the ways they move around them. Layouts with lines, squiggles, zigzags and corners to turn will be explored by children in their own ways. Painted stepping stones, if the gaps are irregular, will encourage children to differentiate between the small and large steps that they need to take.

Grass areas

Children will enjoy playing on grass and begin to notice that running and skipping and hopping feel different and that wheels behave differently on this surface. The softness of grass will encourage rolling, slithering and crawling through barrels and tunnels or directly on the surface. If no grass is available, mats can be used.

Moving to music

Music can be used to suggest certain types of movement to children – sharp and jerky, smooth and flowing, wide and heavy and so on. It can be used to encourage fluidity in movement. When used with a story it can provide an imaginative framework for children to practise a whole range of body skills – roll down the hill, run home quickly, crawl under the blanket. Music can be used to introduce rhythm into children's movement (see chapter ten).

GOOD PRACTICE

Equal opportunities should be a consideration when providing for children's physical development. This should be apparent in the range of activities and in the ways that they are presented. It is also an issue when managing the play. Ensure that all children have access to the activities they choose and that the play is not dominated by physically competent children to the disadvantage of those who are less capable. It may be necessary to limit time on over-subscribed toys – often the new, shiny tricycles – for the sake of fairness. Adults should also challenge, with children, any stereotyping linked to physical play, for example, 'girls can't run fast!'

Ensure that all children have access to equipment and that one group does not dominate

CASE STUDY

Improving outdoor play

The outside play area at the nursery was a fairly small fenced-off part of the primary school playground, adjacent to the nursery. Part of the tarmac surface was covered with a shock-absorbing surface and on this was a climbing frame that was fixed permanently. The nursery had received a substantial amount of money from the parent-teacher association and had spent some of this on a selection of wheeled toys – new tricycles, pedal cars, a trailer and even some bicycles with stabilisers – all of which were proving very popular. The nursery had an outside play period when all children and staff were outside.

The staff felt that the children were not getting as much from outside play as they might. They wanted to do something about this but were not sure what. They asked an NNEB student who was with them to help by observing the outdoor play session over a period of three days and report back. She observed the following.

■ The wheeled toys completely dominated the space and any child or group of children wanting to play with balls were pushed into corners of the playground.

- The younger, newer entrants to nursery were very much on the sidelines of the play and were reluctant to go outside and hung around the door waiting to go in.
- The playground seemed very crowded but the climbing frame which took up a lot of space was hardly used.
- The newer wheeled toys were the focus for squabbles, and staff spent a lot of time mediating in these.
- Staff time was spent on overall supervision and mediating. There was little evidence of adults' extending play.
- Although the session lasted for 40 minutes, some children engaged in no purposeful play during the whole time.
- Any kind of running and jumping type of activity was short-lived and limited by space.
- The play on the wheeled toys was very well developed and almost all children could steer and turn in limited spaces.

    The nursery team discussed the observations and decided on the following, immediate changes.

- Outdoor play was to be available throughout the whole session, with staff to move in and out as numbers of children dictated.
- Wheeled toys were to be put away for a while so that children had a chance to explore other play possibilities on offer. When re-introduced, the number would be limited and a section of the playground would be road-marked for their use.
- Staff would introduce some games to children and offer them on a regular basis.
- Some extension equipment would be bought for the climbing frame in order to make it more interesting to children.
- For a number of sessions every week, an adult would work with the children on developing ball skills.

1 What were the main problems the nursery team were facing here?
2 Do you think these changes will make a significant difference? Why?
3 Could you suggest any other changes that might improve the quality of this nursery's outdoor play?
4 What difficulties do you face in your provision for outdoor play? How might you resolve them?

PROGRESS CHECK

1 What are gross motor skills and what activities are they linked to?
2 Why is physical activity important to children's health?
3 Why should we try to provide regular outdoor play for children?
4 What kinds of physical activities should we provide for children?
5 How can we provide for a range of physical play indoors?

The adult's role in promoting physical development

The adult will play a significant role in promoting physical development in the provision of an environment that allows for practice and consolidation of both fine and gross motor skills and in interacting with individual children to provide challenge and support at appropriate levels. This can be achieved in the following ways.

■ Providing for the full range of abilities in all areas of activity.
■ Interacting with children and helping them to understand and consolidate skills.
■ Acting on observation and 'scaffolding' learning so that the next stage is within reach.
■ Teaching skills, particularly the use of tools.
■ Understanding that skills have to be practised many times and providing for repetition.
■ Recognising confidence as an important component in learning, and supporting children's growing confidence.
■ Introducing vocabulary that enables children to discuss and describe their bodies and their movements.
■ Ensuring safety in the environment and teaching children how to participate in physical play safely.
■ Recognising that equal opportunities is an issue in the provision and management of physical play.

KEY TERMS

You need to know what these words and phrases mean. Go back through the chapter and make sure that you understand:

coordination	practice and refinement
fine motor skills	psychologically
fluidity in movement	'scaffold'
gross motor skills	spatial awareness
manual dexterity	synchronisation
physiologically	

10 CREATIVE DEVELOPMENT

To foster their creative development, children need to acquire skills and be provided with opportunities that enable them to use imagination and express ideas and feelings in a variety of ways. These early experiences will also contribute to their later understanding of art, music, literature, dance and drama.

> *Children explore sound and colour, texture, shape, form and space in two and three dimensions. They respond in a variety of ways to what they see, hear, smell, touch and feel. Through art, music, dance, stories and imaginative play, they show an increasing ability to use their imagination, to listen and to observe. They use a widening range of materials, suitable tools, instruments and other resources to express ideas and to communicate their feelings.*
>
> (Desirable Outcomes for Children's Learning, *DfEE with SCAA, 1996*)

Creativity and individuality

One of the main principles of our approach to the pre-school curriculum is to value the child as an individual and to provide opportunities for the child to discover and develop this individuality. Where adults are involved in encouraging children's creativity, this principle needs to be given due consideration.

WHAT IS CREATIVITY?

Creativity allows for the expressing of ideas and feelings in a personal and unique way. In the adult world we celebrate this creativity in great artistic, literary, musical and dramatic accomplishments and recognise the part that creativity has to play in providing innovative solutions to problems in academic research as well as in inventions. In a more everyday context, the way that we arrange a vase of flowers, decorate a room or put together a meal is also linked to our ability to be creative. Being creative is a uniquely human characteristic involving the expression of imagination in an individual approach to a situation. Children do not need to be taught to be creative but if we want to develop their abilities in this area, we must provide them with opportunities that allow them to explore and experiment, gaining the confidence to express their ideas in a way that is uniquely their own. We facilitate this by providing a rich and stimulating environment that gives children the opportunity to express their feelings about themselves and their world in a variety of ways, and where adults interpret and intervene knowledgeably and sensitively. Children's creativity is not limited to their experiences at the painting easels or at the 'creative' table. It is apparent in many aspects of their lives: in their fantasy and dramatic play, in the way they respond to and make music, in their stories and poems and in their responses to everyday experiences such as flying a kite or playing in the sand.

CREATIVITY AND COMMUNICATION

Children immersed in creative activities will be involved in a process of communication, often with themselves, as well as with others. Here children have an opportunity to re-present, literally, a feeling or an experience in a way that is meaningful to them. Creative experiences offer children a way of refining the way in which they see and understand the world as well as sharing these feelings, responses and imagination with adults and children.

CASE STUDY

Catherine's view of the forest

Catherine, aged four, was fascinated by woods and forests. She had seen a spectacular bluebell display in a wood on a family outing and this seemed to inspire her. She talked about animals that lived in trees, flowers that grew in woods and what it was like to walk through a forest. At storytime she was particularly keen to hear about Little Red Riding Hood and the Three Bears, reflecting on the forest settings.

She came into nursery one day, very keen to get to the easels where, observed by a member of staff, she started on her painting. She provided a running commentary on her painting, placing trees, squirrels, flowers exactly where she thought they should go and taking care with detail and the selection of colour. When she was satisfied that she had included everything that she wanted in her scene, she took a brush fully loaded with black paint and spread it all over her picture, obliterating much of her painstaking detail. She explained to the nursery nurse that it was so dark in her forest, as the trees were so close together, that the sunshine couldn't get through. Catherine was very pleased with her painting and recalled the detail of it to her mother at the end of the session.

1 Why did the nursery nurse stand back and watch Catherine cover her painting with black paint?
2 What does Catherine think are the most important features of forests?
3 What can adults learn from close observation of children engaged in creative activities?

RESPONDING TO CHILDREN'S CREATIVITY

This chapter stresses the importance of recognising the individuality and uniqueness of creativity. If adults are to be successful in supporting the development of children's creativity then they need to communicate to children that they value their endeavours on their own terms, not as inferior to an adult response but as *qualitatively* different from an adult interpretation. Children will not approach their own work with the same confidence and enthusiasm unless they are sure that it will be accepted on its own merits.

CASE STUDY

Making a Mothers' Day card

From a very early age Luke, aged three, loved to draw and paint. He spent hours on these activities at the kitchen table along with making collages and junk modelling. He recently started attending morning sessions at a playgroup and the children were busy making cards for Mothers' Day. Luke was excited at the prospect of making something for his mum and couldn't wait to get started on it. He was pleased with his finished card and took it to show to the playgroup worker. He didn't expect to be told that he hadn't followed the instructions, that he would have to start again and that his mother wouldn't want a card that looked like his. He made another card, closely watched so that it looked like all the others, though he didn't seem so pleased with this one. He didn't seem so eager to stick and paint at the kitchen table any more and when he did he was constantly looking for reassurance that he was doing the right thing.

1 Why do you think the playgroup worker asked Luke to redo his card?
2 What effect has this incident had on Luke's confidence and enthusiasm?
3 How can you make it clear to parents and to children that you value children's creativity for its own sake and not just for the end product?

GOOD PRACTICE

Children need to know that their creative work is accepted for its own worth and uniqueness. If a child is told, for example, that her representation of an elephant doesn't look like an elephant and an adult takes over and draws it for her, the next time that she wants to include an elephant in her painting she may well lack the confidence to attempt it, saying that she cannot do it. This kind of adult intervention undermines and inhibits children's creativity.

PROGRESS CHECK

1 What is creativity?
2 What kinds of activities enable children to explore their creativity?
3 How can adults ensure that they do not inhibit children's creativity?
4 Why are creative activities important to children's development?
5 How is creativity fostered in your workplace?

Providing for children's creativity

Good pre-school provision will ensure that all aspects of children's creative development are catered for. An appropriate environment will encourage children to take part in a wide range of experiences giving them opportunities to explore and experiment. Perhaps even more important than the physical surroundings is the role that staff have to play in supporting children's creative development. Adults should not dominate and stifle children's creativity but, nevertheless, they have a vital part to play.

Adults can support children's creativity in many ways.

- Providing an environment that is rich and stimulating.
- Presenting activities in an attractive and appropriate way.
- Making interesting and appropriate materials available.
- Valuing children's individual interpretations and responses.
- Having realistic expectations of the children's capabilities.
- Giving creativity priority. This includes giving time to planning and evaluation as well as to implementation.
- Teaching skills and techniques that can be used in creative work, such as paint mixing, sticking, cutting and sewing.

Children need to be taught skills that can be used in their own creative work

- Giving time to children, showing interest and encouragement on an individual basis.
- Showing children that you value their work through the emphasis you give to it in displays.
- Providing opportunities for children to talk about work with other children, staff and visitors.

GOOD PRACTICE

Displays in the centre can communicate to children, parents and visitors that you value children's own work. Thoughtfully mounted and organised, children's paintings, drawings, collage and models demonstrate the approach and philosophy of the centre as well as looking attractive and providing an interesting focus.

DRAWING AND PAINTING

By the time they come to the childcare centre, children are likely to have had widely varying experiences of drawing and painting. Most children will have had opportunities to use different types of drawing media and many will be familiar with paint too. However it is not helpful to assume that all children have had common experiences. There is a developmental sequence attached to children's drawing and painting and although this is linked to developmental age, it is also dependent on exposure to the media and practice. The following stages trace the development of drawing from approximately twelve months to around four or five years.

Drawing – stages of development
- Before ever coming into contact with a crayon or pencil, children will probably scribble with fingers in soft food, sand or on steamy windows.
- When presented with a crayon children will often explore with the mouth. They may make marks, probably incidentally, showing little interest in them.
- Control is being gained, and scribble (a) (see page 182) progresses through vertical and lateral (b) to circular (c).
- The oval shape isolated from scribble, is repeated at will (d).
- The oval becomes 'big-head' shape decorated with marks and lines, like radials of the sun (e).
- Radials are reduced, those remaining resemble limbs sticking out of big-head figure (f, g).
- The head now has long hairpin legs, sometimes closed to form a body (h, i).
- The figure is often presented with a triangular or square body (j, k).
- Limbs are presented as loops (l).
- Details are added to the figures.
- Background begins to be noted, 'strip' sky and ground appear.
- The child will often draw what he knows, not what he sees, for example he knows people are likely to be inside a house so when he draws a house he draws the occupants too, even though he couldn't see them from outside.

This sequence will be more apparent in drawings than in paintings, but once established these representations of figures will appear in paintings too.

(a) Random scribble

(b) Lateral vertical scribble

(c) Emerging oval

(d) Oval

(e) Radial

(f) Big head

(g) Big head

(h) Hairpin figure

(i) Filled in hairpin figure

(j) Bighead and triangle

(k) Amorphous figure

(l) Loop or sausage figure

The development sequence of drawing

Painting – stages of development

Paint is a different medium and presents children with other challenges and possibilities. A developmental sequence in painting can also be observed (see page 184) as children get to grips with the medium.

(see page 184)

CASE STUDY

Nathan's painting

Four-year-old Nathan was a newcomer to nursery. He lived with his parents and baby sister in a bed and breakfast hotel. He was a lively and interested child but at the painting table he was engrossed in covering sheet after sheet with paint applied in large scrubbing movements, covering the paper, the table and often himself. He took little interest in the finished product but moved it away and started on the next sheet. The nursery staff had noticed his behaviour and discussed him at their next meeting.

1 Would you be concerned about Nathan's painting?
2 Could you think of some reasons why Nathan paints in this way?
3 How would you respond?

Providing for drawing

A variety of drawing media will allow children to discover different properties and applications. The following would provide a range of effects.

- Pencils: thick and thin, carbon and coloured.
- Charcoal: show the techniques associated with the medium.
- Chalk: white and coloured offer different effects and textures.
- Crayons: different thicknesses and textures.
- Felt and fibre tip pens: provide a wide range, including those that blend together.
- Pastels: oil and water pastels provide a wide range of effects though they are expensive and fragile.

Providing for painting

The way that painting is provided for will depend on the space available and, to some extent, on the budget. With this in mind, here are some general points.

- Provide a variety of paints.
  - Powder paint is versatile, can be mixed to different consistencies and can be mixed with PVA glue for different effects. It is convenient when ready mixed for the children in non-spill pots but children will enjoy mixing colours to different strengths themselves, dabbing a wet brush into the dry powder and then onto the paper or mixing colours on a palette. This may be more messy but offers a whole range of possibilities with it.
  - Redimix paint in squeezy bottles is more expensive and less versatile but it is convenient, easy to store and particularly good in fluorescent colours.
  - Finger paints can be made cheaply at the centre with powder paint and starch. They are also available commercially.

Around 18 months	2 years	3 years	4 years	5 years
Whole arm movements. Very few strokes on a page. Shifting of brush from one hand to the other. Satisfied with one colour.	More wrist action than before. Fewer shifts in handedness though might paint with a brush in each hand. Scrubbing action with little regard for colour. Paints several colours over each other with muddy effect, often makes holes in the paper. Experiments with vertical and horizontal lines, dots and circular movements. Doesn't keep within boundaries – paints table, floor, self. Involved in process, not much regard for end product.	Strokes are varied and rhythmical. Some beginning of design evident. Patch painting emerges – colours whole paper with one colour or blocks of colour. Knows what he's painting but this is often not recognisable. More concern for the finished product. More concentration and detail evident.	Holds brush in an adult manner. Design more apparent, often includes letters from name. Ideas often modified during the process of painting e.g. the robot becomes a spaceship. Verbal commentary. Explains and justifies his actions to himself. Personal pride in painting.	Usually holds on to initial idea. Figures, subjects usually recognisable. Detail is increasing (linked to provision and practice). Most important details are drawn largest. Chooses colour deliberately. Sometimes dissatisfied with attempts to portray ideas.

The development sequence in painting

- Provide a variety of brushes and tools.
  - Provide a range of thick to thin brushes as this enables a variety of effects. Decorators' brushes are useful for large areas. Brushes need care: those in poor condition will not perform adequately.
  - Introduce tools that can be used with paint such as sponges, corks, old toothbrushes and straws, and demonstrate how to use these techniques.
- Provide a variety of papers.
  - Give children the chance to experiment with paint on different surfaces, smooth, rough, shiny, corrugated. Scrap paper can be obtained at little or no cost from a variety of sources.
  - Provide paper in a range of colours to choose from. If children are representing themselves, make available paper that reflects their skin tones.
  - Cut paper to different sizes and shapes and give children a chance to select.
- Furniture. Try to offer easels as well as tables for painting so that children can discover how paint behaves in a vertical plane. Large scale works often need to take over some floor space. Think about how you can store paintings during their fragile, wet stage.

GOOD PRACTICE

Introduce children to different artists' work and artistic styles. Children will enjoy looking at prints, talking about colour, subject matter and technique. Their own work may well begin reflect what they see and discuss. Ensure that the examples you choose reflect cultural diversity, representing art from many traditions, not just those that you are most familiar with. If possible, invite artists in to talk about their work and perhaps to do some work with the children.

CASE STUDY

Painting sunflowers

The children in the nursery had grown some sunflowers from seed as part of a science topic. Observational drawing was encouraged in the nursery and the sunflowers seemed ideal subjects. The children talked about the flower-heads, noticing the colours, the size and the way the heads nodded with the weight of the seeds. The children made their own drawings using pencils, charcoal and pastels. They were introduced to a print of Van Gogh's *Sunflowers*, again talking about the colours and noticing the thickness of the paint. Inspired by this, many of them went on to paint their own observed sunflowers 'in the style of Van Gogh'. The influence was clear in the way the children chose bright colours and used thick paint. The children's work was displayed alongside the print.

1 The children in this example were inspired by the painting. What is the difference between this and copying?
2 Why do you think this was such a successful activity?
3 What do childcare workers need to do when planning activities like this?

The children painted their sunflowers in the style of Van Gogh

COLLAGE

Collage involves sticking two or three dimensional materials such as fabrics, paper, boxes, twigs, feathers etc. and will thus introduce children to a variety of textures. To begin with, children are likely to be interested as much in the glue and its properties as what and where they are sticking. This is normal: the children need to find out all about glue before they will think more readily about what they are going to stick on with the glue. As their experience increases they will move from random selection and positioning of materials to carefully planned and executed designs sometimes using the collage material realistically in their pictures, for example choosing feathers for a picture of a bird.

Providing for collage
- Supply the appropriate adhesive. Children would soon become frustrated trying to stick carpet with wallpaper paste!
- Collect and store a wide range of collage materials. Ask parents and children to help.
- Organise storage so that materials are accessible to children. (**NB** Ensure all materials are safe.)
- Collage materials can be 'themed', for example natural materials or shiny things. Choosing from within a theme can provide a framework for children's work.
- Provide a variety of surfaces for children to stick onto – card, board, fabric, etc.
- Teach children how to use different tearing and cutting techniques and provide scissors that are effective. Include left-handed scissors too.

- Collage can provide children with opportunities to make interesting discoveries about colour mixing. Overlapping tissue paper or cellophane will show how colours are comprised.

BOX AND JUNK MODELLING

Working in three dimensions presents another challenge to children's creativity. At the early stages, children will be happy to group boxes together with little evidence of a design. As they become more practised in the techniques associated with modelling, design and intention become more apparent. They move from a seemingly random combination to careful selection of materials and realisation of a design.

Providing for modelling
- Collect enough materials to allow the children maximum flexibility.
- Store these in an organised and accessible way.
- Demonstrate and resource a variety of joining techniques. Gluing is only one way; children will enjoy using sellotape, treasury tags, staples, cutting flaps and making hinges.
- Provide enough space and time for the activity.
- Protect the models when they are at their most fragile i.e. when wet.

CLAY, DOUGH AND OTHER MALLEABLE MATERIALS

These experiences can provide another means of creative expression. Children will need to familiarise themselves with these materials before they become aware of their potential. They will practise techniques of cutting and rolling and experiment with tools. They will take great pleasure making something, admiring it, modifying it and then squashing it and starting again. They can combine these materials with others with different qualities such as pebbles, fir cones and shells. Baking and firing can extend the activity further.

GOOD PRACTICE

If we want to ensure that children get the most from the activities we provide for them we need to consider the way in which they are presented. Activities should be set up with their learning potential in mind and sited appropriately Areas should be arranged invitingly so that the children are drawn into them. Sometimes presenting a familiar activity in an unexpected way will do this. The activities should be maintained during the session so materials should always be available. An adult should be on hand ready to support and develop the learning that is taking place.

MUSIC

The pre-school environment should provide opportunities for children to listen and respond to music and to make their own music. You do not have to be a music specialist or be skilled with an instrument to provide for this aspect of children's creative development. Exceptionally, children of three and four will be learning to play instruments but for most children the aim of these early musical experiences is to open another channel for communication and self-expression and, from these early years, to foster an appreciation of music.

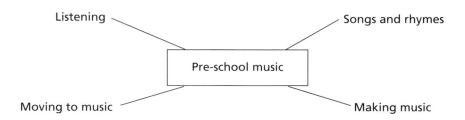

Listening
- Everyday environments can be noisy and it may be necessary to practice listening to enable children to respond to music. Listening walks provide a good focus for this as do tapes of everyday sounds. You can also get children to identify outside sounds from inside. This seems to work particularly well if children close their eyes and try to identify individual sounds from the general outside hum.
- Make listening to music part of your everyday programme. Introduce a wide range of musical styles to children at small group time. Choose music that is culturally diverse, classical and contemporary, including electronic. Encourage requests and music from home. Choose excerpts carefully, not too long, and repeat them so that children become familiar with them and begin to recognise them. Identify the characteristics of music – pace, tone, pitch – and listen for phrases that recur.
- Provide a listening centre using cassette players and headphones. Children enjoy handling the equipment independently. Junction boxes allow a number of headphones to be connected to the same cassette player. (**NB** Ensure that the volume is set at a safe level.)
- Invite someone who plays an instrument into your group, maybe a parent or an older child. Sometimes professional musicians are available locally as part of Arts in the Community programmes

Songs and rhymes
- Teach rhymes and songs. Children will respond from a very early age.
- Include actions with your rhymes. It will help children concentrate and aid memory.
- Choose all sorts of rhymes – traditional, funny, number – and from all over the world.
- In your song and rhyme time, try for a balance between old favourites and new songs. Make time for requests.
- Alert children to rhythm in songs and rhymes. Introduce clapping and simple musical accompaniment.

- Get children to use their voices musically. Singing 'Good morning' or their names at register time can work very well.
- These experiences provide children with opportunities to learn about tune, rhythm, timing and pattern in music.

Moving to music
- Create a mood with music. Choose sad music, cheerful music, frightening music, etc. and get the children to respond.
- Set a scene with music. A mixture of sounds and tunes can represent say, the sea or the rainforest.
- Use music to tell a story. Different pieces of music can be associated with characters and events in the story. 'Peter and the Wolf' and 'The Carnival of Animals' are old favourites here but the approach works with other music, too.
- Give children an opportunity to respond physically to music. They need space and time to develop confidence in dance. Involve all children but be aware that some may be shyer than others.
- Introduce children to different styles of dance. Community dance groups will often perform for children.

Making music
- Encourage children to make their own home-made instruments, including those to shake, pluck, blow and scrape. Provide a range of materials for fillings and twanging so that children can identify different sounds in the same musical family.

Give children an opportunity to make their own music

- Provide commercially available instruments for children to use alongside their home-made ones. Try to represent all musical traditions.
- Explore music made from body sounds – clapping, tapping, clicking – and examine voice sounds.
- Use music to accompany stories when you tell them and encourage children to do the same with their own stories and imaginative play.
- Hold musical conversations where children respond with their instruments or clapping. Get them tapping (or shaking, or twanging) a rhythm or repeating a regular pattern.
- Let children tape their music to share with parents or to use in their play.
- Introduce the concept of musical notation. Some children may already be familiar with this and might be keen to devise their own methods for writing down their rhythms.

CASE STUDY

Chinese New Year

Children in the nursery had been preparing for the Chinese New Year celebrations. Musicians from the local Chinese community centre had been invited into school. The children had a wonderful afternoon listening to some unfamiliar instruments and rhythms and watching dancing. The musicians brought in many instruments and the children were encouraged to hold them and, when they felt ready, to join in with the music. The children were then shown how to do simple dance steps and many of them joined in with the performance. Later that week, the nursery held its own Lion Dance parade to celebrate the Chinese New Year. They used their instruments to tap out the rhythms that they had practised earlier and some even remembered the dance steps.

1 What was valuable about this experience for the children?
2 Can you think of ways in which work like this might be extended or followed up?
3 Can you think of any resources in your area that might be available to enrich the curriculum in this kind of way?

IMAGINATIVE AND DRAMATIC PLAY

All pre-school settings will plan for a range of imaginative play opportunities. Most will provide an area for domestic play alongside other provision for imaginative role play such as a café or a hospital. Children will be able to create their own scenarios in large and small brick apparatus and in small world play. Dressing-up clothes may be available in role play areas, fitting in with the theme, or this may be presented as a separate activity in its own right. Sand and water and other messy activities may also provide a focus for children's imaginative play. Books and stories provide a stimulus to the imagination as stories are recalled and replayed with the child's own emphasis and pace. But if you observe children of this age for any length of time you will notice that there is also much imaginative and creative play that falls into none of these planned areas.

Children's ability to use symbols in their imaginative play develops from around the age of two years. By three or four they can respond to these symbols in a quite sophisticated way. A child picking up a piece of ragged curtain can very soon turn it into a fast-flowing river convincing himself that he will get washed away if he tries to cross it. Other children may join in with the fantasy and become completely involved. However, the curtain does not stay a river for ever and when you next overhear the children's conversation it will have become, say, a spaceship or a dog or a mountain.

Imaginative play is extremely important to young children's development. It allows them to develop this ability to use symbols, and through this play they learn more about social roles and become more aware of themselves. Like painting and drawing, it can provide them with a means of communication, with others and with themselves and also provide them with another perspective on the world and their role in it.

CASE STUDY

Hospital play

Liam was preparing for a planned admission to hospital. Quite a few children were in a similar situation and the nursery staff had set up an imaginative play area based on a hospital ward. This contained white coats, stethoscopes and medical equipment. Liam spent a lot of time on the ward, sometimes as a doctor or nurse, sometimes as the patient. He was very interested in the equipment, particularly the syringes. The nursery nurse observed him with another child. Liam was taking the role of the doctor, syringe in hand, telling his friend that he didn't need to cry, that it wouldn't hurt at all.

1 What is the value of this type of play, to Liam or to any child?
2 Can you think of other situations where imaginative play might help a child who was troubled about something? How could you provide for this?

Providing for imaginative play

- Domestic play is popular with most pre-school aged children. Vary your home corner provision maintaining the balance between familiar and new attractions.
- Plan for other imaginative play areas perhaps linking with any theme that you may be developing.
- Dressing-up clothes need to be easy to put on. Provide hats, bags and other accessories. Children enjoy admiring themselves in a mirror.
- Make time and space for large plastic or wooden brick play. This often involves collaboration and complex story lines.
- Show children that you value their imaginative play by talking to them about it. Get them to talk to the others during group time.
- Present small world play in varied ways, sometimes on playmats, sometimes in the sand, sometimes in with the plastic or wooden bricks.

Children will enjoy admiring themselves in a mirror

- Guard against stereotypical expectations of what particular groups should or should not do. Use imaginative play to challenge stereotypes.
- Join in children's imaginative play. Don't take it over but extend and challenge sensitively.
- Plan for imaginative play outside too. Some markings on the play surface can trigger all kinds of games. Chalk washes away in the rain and you can change it next time.
- Provide for children's special needs. Make sure that imaginative play can be enjoyed by all members of the group.
- Reflect cultural diversity in your home corner provision. If you introduce anything unfamiliar to the children – food, clothes, cooking utensils – demonstrate how it would be used.
- Give children plenty of time and space to develop their own imaginative play. Encourage them to use resources in their own unique ways.

THE ADULT'S ROLE

To sum up, the adult's role in supporting creative development is to provide children with access to a range of learning opportunities that are appropriately resourced in terms of materials, staff, time and space. Skills and techniques that complement creativity will need to be taught so that new options can be explored. Children need a climate that values their work in an environment that is stimulating and enabling and that meets their individual needs. A skilful adult responds sensitively and is able to assess how to challenge and extend the child towards the next level of understanding.

GOOD PRACTICE

The needs of all children must be considered when planning for children's creativity. Ensure that you are providing a range that meets the needs of all in the group. Consider whether some provision needs to be differentiated to make it available to children with particular needs.

PROGRESS CHECK

1 Make a list of points that you should consider when providing for children's creativity.
2 Observe your workplace during a typical session. What opportunities are you providing for children to develop their creativity?

KEY TERMS

You need to know what these words and phrases mean. Go back through the chapter and make sure that you understand:

collage
creativity
cultural diversity
drawing media
imaginative role play
individuality

learning potential
malleable materials
observational drawing
patch painting
social roles
symbolic play

Further reading

Jameson, K., *Pre-school and Infant Art*, Studio Vista, 1974

GLOSSARY

The following words or phrases appear as key terms at the ends of chapters. A brief explanation of each as it relates to the pre-school curriculum is given here.

Base-line assessment
An assessment of the child's capabilities on entry to the centre. This may be centre- or LEA-devised. There is a move to introduce a standard base-line assessment nationally for five-year-olds.

Child-centred approach
The development of a curriculum that takes children's needs and abilities as its starting point.

Creativity
The ability to express ideas and feelings in an original way using the imagination.

Cultural diversity
The fact that a number of different traditions and cultures contribute to our national identity.

Curriculum
This is defined in its broadest sense as a course of study. In the context of the pre-school environment a consideration of how children learn, as well as what they learn, is essential. It should also be noted that the curriculum transmits attitudes and values as well as knowledge.

Desirable Outcomes
Guidance on curriculum content issued by the Department for Education and Employment in 1996 and linked to government funding of the education of four-year-olds. The desirable outcomes should be achieved by the average child on admission to compulsory education at five.

Differentiation
The matching of provision to the individual needs and developmental level of the child.

Developmentally appropriate
An understanding that provision, interaction and expectations should be linked to the child's level of development.

Equal opportunities
An approach to working with people that seeks to ensure that all have fair chances while recognising that some groups are more likely to be disadvantaged than others.

Integrated learning
An approach to the curriculum that does not emphasise artificial distinctions between different subject areas.

Interaction
Any kind of exchange or communication between individuals.

Intervention
In the context of the pre-school environment, intervention is used to describe an adult becoming involved with children with a particular purpose in mind.

Learning potential
In the context of this book, this is taken to mean the range of possible learning that an activity or experience might provide for the child.

Monitoring and evaluation
Scrutiny of the educational process that enables practitioners to assess and draw conclusions about the effectiveness of their practice.

National Curriculum
The curriculum prescribed for all state schools in England and Wales for children aged between five and sixteen. It was introduced in 1988 as part of the Education Reform Act and requires that children are tested at the end of each Key Stage of their school career.

Portfolio
A collection of a child's work over a period of time which documents individual progress.

Positive images
Extending and increasing expectations through the presentation of images that challenge stereotypes.

Professional development
The ongoing updating of skills and knowledge that is required for successful professional practice.

Role-modelling
The process through which children observe adult responses and attitudes and assimilate them into their own behaviour.

Self-esteem
An individual's assessment of their own worth.

Stereotypes
A fixed belief about the characteristics or capabilities of individuals because they belong to a particular group. Stereotypes are often applied on the basis of race, sex or disability.

Tokenistic
The superficial representation of minority groups, for example including a single black child in a prospectus.

FURTHER READING

Abbot, L. and Rodger, R., *Quality Education in the Early Years,* Open University Press, 1994

Anning, A., *A National Curriculum for the Early Years*, Open University Press, 1995

Beaver, M. et al., *Babies and Young Children, Book One, Development*, Stanley Thornes (Publishers) Ltd, 1994

Beaver, M. et al., *Babies and Young Children, Book Two, Work and Care*, Stanley Thornes (Publishers) Ltd, 1995

Browne, N. and France, P.,*Untying the Apron Strings*, Open University Press, 1986

Bruce, T., *Early Childhood Education*, Hodder & Stoughton, 1987

Campbell, R., *Reading Real Books*, Open University Press, 1992

Carlgren, F., *Education Towards Freedom*, Lanthorn Press, 1972

Curtis, A., *A Curriculum for the Pre-school Child*, NFER- Nelson, 1986

Davenport, G.C., *An Introduction to Child Development*, Unwin Hyman, 1988

DfEE, *Nursery Education Scheme: The Next Steps*, DfEE, 1996

DfEE with SCAA, *Desirable Outcomes for Children's Learning*, DfEE, 1996

Dixon, B., *Playing Them False*, Trenthan, 1989

Dowling, M., *Education 3-5*, Paul Chapman Publishers, 1988

Early Years Curriculum Group, *The Early Years Curriculum – and the National Curriculum*, Trentham Books, 1995

Edwards, A. and Knight, P., *Effective Early Years Education*, Open University Press, 1994

Hughes, M., *Children and Number,* Blackwell, 1986

Hurst, V., *Planning for Early Learning,* Paul Chapman Publishers,1991

Jameson, K., *Pre-school and Infant Art*, Studio Vista, 1974

Maccoby, E., *Psychological Growth and the Parent Child Relationship,* Harcourt Brace Jovanovich, 1980

Manning, K. and Sharp, A., *Structuring Play in the Early Years,* Ward Locke, 1977

Matusiak, C., *Foundations for the Early Years*, Scholastic Publications Ltd, 1992

Meadows, S. and Cashdan, A., *Helping Children Learn*, David Fulton Press, 1988

Miller, D., *Children and Race*, Ward Locke, 1983

Moyles, J.,*Just Playing*, Open University Press, 1989

Moyles, J., *The Excellence of Play*, Open University Press, 1995

Neaum, S., *High Scope*, University of Nottingham, 1993

Osborne, A.F. and Milbank, J.E., *The Effects of Early Years Education*, Clarendon Press, 1987

The Plowden Report, *Children and their Primary Schools*, HMSO, 1967

Pugh, G., *Contemporary Issues in the Early Years*, Paul Chapman Press, 1996

Richards, R. and Jones, L., *An Early Start to Mathematics*, Simon Schuster, 1990

The Rumbold Report, *Starting with Quality*, HMSO, 1990

Smith, E., *Educating the Under Fives*, Cassell, 1994

Sutherland, P., *Cognitive Development Today, Piaget and his critics*, Paul Chapman Press, 1992

Whitehead, M., *Language and Literacy in the Early Years*, Paul Chapman Press, 1990

USEFUL ADDRESSES

The British Association for Early Childhood Education (BAECE)
111 City View House
463 Bethnal Green Road
London E2 9QR
Tel. 0171 739 7594

Childsplay (Multi-cultural toy shop)
112 Tooting High Street
London SW17 0RR
Tel. 0181 672 6470

Commission for Racial Equality
Elliot House
10-12 Allington street
London SW1E 5EH
Tel. 0171 828 7088

Daycare Trust/National Childcare Campaign [NCCC]
Wesley House
4 Wild Court
London WC2B 4AU
Tel. 0171 405 5617/8

National Campaign for Nursery Education [NCNE]
BCM Box 6216
London WC1N 3XX

National Children's Bureau – Early Childhood Unit
8 Wakely Street
London EC1V 7QE
Tel. 0171 843 6000

National Early Years Network
77 Holloway Road
London N7 8JZ
Tel. 0171 607 9573

Nottingham Educational Supplies
Ludlow Hill Road
West Bridgford
Nottingham NG2 6HD
Tel. 0115 945 2200

Pre-school Learning Alliance
69 Kings Cross Road
London WC1X 9LL
Tel. 0171 833 0991

Working Group against Racism in Children's Resources (WGARCR)
Lady Margaret Settlement
460 Wandsworth Road
London SW8 3LX
Tel. 0171 627 4594

INDEX